I0474112

DARKROOM DATAGUIDE

By

Peter Martin Jones

Contents

Introduction

A number of books have been published on darkroom technique that explains all the basic elements involved from processing the film through to toning prints etc.

Many of these books are excellent and provide a good source of reference for the darkroom worker. Indeed every darkroom worker should find space on their book-shelves for one or two such books to browse through or consult at leisure.

The Darkroom Data Guide however, is not basically a "how to do it" book, al-though many hints and tips have been included not found elsewhere.

It is primarily a compact but comprehensive collection of information and data that can be consulted instantly in the darkroom. Detailed fault finding charts have been included to identify the cause and rectification of processing and printing problems for both colour and black and white. There are also dilution tables, ex-posure compensation tables, conversion tables, Multigrade filter values and many other facts and tables that will provide an invaluable reference source.

The whole purpose of the guide is for information to be available quickly to re-solve problems and remove the drudgery of tedious calculations. Above all else it is designed for speed and to prevent the searching for information that often oc-curs when a problem arises.

We hope you will find the Darkroom Data Guide an indispensable item that gives more time for processing and printing. After all, that's what the darkroom is for.

One of the fascinations of photography is that you never stop learning, and dark-room work is certainly no exception. There are many times when a "new" discov-ery will present itself and it is essential to note these down for future reference.

In order to make this easier we have included blank sets of tables for you to do this. For example, you may find the reason for a particular fault occurring on a colour print, which we have not listed. In the event of this occurring simply enter the information into the table to extend it.

In this way you will build up a very valuable personalized data file - all contained in one book. Similarly we have left some blank pages at the end of the book for you to make your own notes.

There are many variables involved in processing film and papers in the darkroom. Process time, temperature and agitation technique are just a few parameters, which can affect your results.

Consistency and cleanliness are the watchwords for good results. If you stan-dardize your technique you are 90% of the way there. If you find a good film/developer combination, stick with it and use exactly the same dilutions, temperatures and processing times etc every time.

Experiment by all means if you wish to, but if the film is an important one, stay with your tried and tested techniques. Always make a note of any discovery or new useful information you come across. You may curse yourself later if you don't.

Please take the time to read the section on Home Processing even if you have processed a number of films already. This topic includes a large number of tips and wrinkles that may provide some new ideas for even experienced darkroom workers.

Successful printing and processing will be assured if you abide by the following:

Materials and chemicals

Make sure you use only chemical and other materials that are good quality and that are in date.

Equipment

All equipment you use should be of sufficient quality. Enlargers should have rigid columns and the enlarging lens should be the correct focal length (50mm for 35mm negatives and 80mm for 6 x 6 negatives.

Cleanliness

This is most important. All dishes tanks etc **must** be clean otherwise cross contamination will result ruining your results. **Never** vacuum clean or dust your darkroom area just before using it. Dust will rise up into the area and descend like radioactive fallout over everything for several hours.

Consistency

Always be consistent with all chemical processing times and don't vary them from film to film. If you get a good result – note the processing details down (in this book) for use later

Accuracy

For good results all solutions should be at the correct temperature and maintained throughout the processing period. Dilutions also must be accurate.

****

Remember- if you abide by these rules your results will be reliable and you will be able to repeat them in the future.

Experiment by all means. But if you do then note the results down in this book for future reference. If you do this you can repeat the exact same procedure next time. All scientific laboratories do this and we should do the same.

Health and Safety

- Wear eye protection while mixing solutions and wear rubber gloves.

- Do not allow chemical contact with skin.

- Chemical combinations can produce harmful vapours so ensure you work in a very well ventilated room.

- Keep all chemicals in labeled bottles, preferably with childproof caps and definitely out of reach of children or pets.

- Use a funnel to pour mixtures into a bottle

- Do not store solutions in high temperatures or sunlight.

- Do not pour chemicals down the drain unless they are heavily diluted with water. Check with your local environment officer to advise the best procedure for disposing of chemicals.

- Always add powders or liquids to the water to avoid powders being lumpy and liquids spitting.

- Wipe up spills immediately to avoid staining or damage to surfaces

- Avoid breathing in the fumes from any chemicals.

- Stick with recognized formulas if mixing your own chemicals and do not try to create your own formulas unless you know exactly what you are doing.

Film Processing

The term home processing implies to many people, rank amateurs achieving medio-cre results from a cupboard under the stairs and that the standards achieved are considerably inferior to those produced by professional laboratories.

Whilst this may be true in some cases, a very large proportion of "Home Proces-sors" achieve outstanding results rivaling or even exceeding professional hand print-ers. Why do I say this? Well here are a few of the many reasons:

- Professional printers cannot spend too much time on printing and processing each print – otherwise they won't make any money, whereas the amateur of-ten spends a considerable amount of time to achieve a particular result.

- Advanced amateurs normally use fresh chemicals as opposed to the replen-ishing techniques used by professionals.

- Having taken the original picture on film, the amateur knows the effect they are after and can carry this through to the processing or enlarging stage.

- Dare I mention mass processing high street labs where your prints are re-turned with stickers telling you how to avoid a problem from a "poor print" next time. Fine but this shot may well have been a "special effects shot" that their automated systems can't deal with.

Apart from this, the amateur can save time and money and still get top quality re-sults by processing their own films and prints.

Equipment Required

Before you process an exposed film you need the following items:

Changing Bag

A changing bag is a bit like a T-shirt with a zip across the waist and elasticated sleeves. It is made out of light tight material and has a second inner compartment also with a zip. The sleeves fit tightly around your arms making the whole bag light tight. Films needs to be loaded into the light tight developing tank in complete dark-ness and the changing bag offers a convenient, reliable, cheap and portable option to do this.

You can produce a makeshift changing bag using a heavy coat or dive under the bed sheets providing, in both cases, that the materials are thick enough to prevent light seeping through.

Alternatively, find a room in the house that can be blacked out easily. In each case test the room for light proofness by allowing about 15 minutes for your eyes to adjust. If it's still pitch black it's safe enough to load the film. If it's not the film will be light fogged and even slight fogging will deteriorate the image.

Developing Tank

This is a water and light type tank designed to hold films that are preloaded on spiral reels ready for processing. The lid is specially designed to allow chemicals to be poured in without light reaching the films and when the lid is refitted the tank can be inverted without chemicals spilling out. These essential features ensure all films receive even development in complete darkness

You could develop the film in any light tight container, but you'd have to lift off the lid in complete darkness to pour in chemicals. You could also develop the film in a container in the darkroom but in both cases ensuring even development can be tricky and definitely not recommended. Stick with the developing tank. It is time tested and gives good consistent results.

Thermometer

One of the most critical aspects of film processing is to ensure that the chemicals are at the correct temperature and maintained at this temperature. It's vital that the developer temperature is measured accurately otherwise you may produce thin or dense negatives that are unprintable. The thermometer must be of good quality and sufficiently accurate for processing. Photographic quality thermometers are stocked by most darkroom suppliers.

Some people are very good at guesstimating temperature but this is not accurate enough for good consistent results. Please don't do it!

Scissors

Film is attached to its spool inside the cassette with strong tape. It's easier to cut the film off rather than try to unpeel the tape. It also helps loading the film into the spiral if the tapered part of the film leader is cut off. Any household scissors are suitable providing they are sharp.

Darkroom Timer

It's important that the time the film is immersed in developer is measured accurately to ensure the film is correctly processed. You should use a timer that measures in seconds, preferably one with a minute counter too so you can keep track of the overall processing time as well as the agitation time within each stage. If your clock or watch has a second's hand you can use that.

Darkroom Data Guide

Developers

A developer reacts with the exposed areas of silver in the film turning these parts black to form an image. Areas that receive more light become blacker when developed. Areas that receive no light stay clear. You have to use a developer to produce a result.

You can make up your own developers for black and white films. See the section 'mixing your own chemicals'

Funnels

A selection of small funnels is very useful for pouring chemicals into bottles etc. The translucent Polypropylene variety are very good.

Stop Baths

This is an acid solution that quickly counteracts the developer to prevent over development of the film. You can use water but it doesn't stop the developer as quickly. As it is acetic acid some people use vinegar, but it's not recommended. It is a poor substitute.

Fixers

This dissolves any unused silver halides and other chemicals that were not developed and stops the film from being light sensitive. You have to use a fixer otherwise the negative will eventually degrade. You can also make up your own fixer. See the section "mixing your own chemicals"

Measuring Chemicals

Most chemicals need diluting before use. The dilutions necessary can be difficult to measure without accurate measuring cylinders, especially when the chemical to water ratio is large. See the Dilution Tables in this book.

Any plastic household measuring jug can be used providing it has the necessary measuring graduations on it. Polypropylene is best .You must not then re-use the jug for food because the chemicals used for processing are harmful. However measuring cylinders are more accurate. Use these if you can.

The best way of measuring out small quantities of liquid chemicals is to use a plastic hypodermic syringe. This is particularly effective for syrupy mixtures. It is clean quick and accurate that's why they use them in medicine.

Washing

Washing is required to ensure that all traces of fixer are removed before the film is hung up to dry. It is preferable to use a washing hose that fits on the bathroom tap and also plugs into the developing tank. These units are also sold with an in line filter to ensure no foreign particles get onto the film emulsion.

It's possible to wash a film with just a bucket of water. Some photographers use just enough water to fill the tank ten times, but the more water you use the less likely you'll leave any traces of fixer behind on the film.

Rinsing with Wetting Agent

This is an important stage that should be carried out before drying the film. After washing, immerse the film in a solution of water and a wetting agent (like Ilford Ilfotol). This breaks down the surface tension of the water and allows the film dry with a lesser chance of drying marks

Drying

A clip is attached to each side of the film to hang it up to dry. The one at the bottom is weighted to stretch the film and ensure it dries evenly. Plastic or wooden clothes pegs can be used and are just as effective. Use two or three pegs at the bottom to add weight (add some blue tack if necessary) and pull the film taught. If the film is not hung taught it might curl up on itself after it dries.

Film Retriever

A film retriever is a gadget that you use to pull out the film's leader when it has been wound into the cassette You slide the metal strip of the retriever into the film's light trap and a grip hooks on to the sprockets of the film so it can be extracted from the cassette.

However, if you have a camera with a manual rewind it's easy to leave the leader out when you rewind the film. Cameras with auto rewind can often be prevented from fully winding the leader into the canister by listening for the film clicking off the take up spool and opening the back as you hear this.

In an emergency it's also possible to retrieve a leader by wetting the leader from another film pushing it in and waiting a few minutes for the films to stick together, then if you're really careful you can pull both out together.

Otherwise in total darkness use a bottle opener to remove the top lid of the cassette and carefully pull the film out of it.

Thermometers

A good quality thermometer is essential for accurate control of processing solutions. Buy a photographic quality thermometer from a Darkroom supplier.

Gloves

Wear cotton gloves to avoid finger marks or scratches when handling the dry film. If you don't want to wear gloves wash your hands and then thoroughly dry them before handling the film to prevent grease or dust being transferred to it.

Always wear protective plastic or latex disposable gloves to protect your hands when handling chemicals.

Film Squeegees

These are used to remove most of the water off the film surface so that it can dry quickly without marks. Alternatively you can use two fingers and draw your fingers down the film. I prefer the fingers approach out of the two. With either method make sure there are no traces of dust or grit on the surface of the squeegee or your fingers, as this will create a long irreparable scratch as you run down the length of film.

Whether using a squeegee or your fingers, dip them into your final rinsing solution and shake off the excess liquid first before applying them to the film. It is more likely that you will get drying marks on the film if you do not wipe the film.

Note: Wipe the film once only. Under no circumstances do it twice. The odds are you will damage the film emulsion if you do. Don't be tempted even if you see a few drops of water left on the film. I have been there and done that!

Processing Procedure

Lets start at the beginning. Before you can process your film you must first load it into your developing tank. Sound's simple but sometimes it can be difficult with the film jamming or sticking in the spirals. This is how it should be done.

The following notes are based on processing black and white films for the sake of brevity but the same basic procedure applies to processing all films.

Film Loading

Retrieve the film leader as described above and then cut off the end of the film square followed by cutting the corners of the film off. This makes loading the film in the spiral very much easier. Do not cut through a sprocket hole.

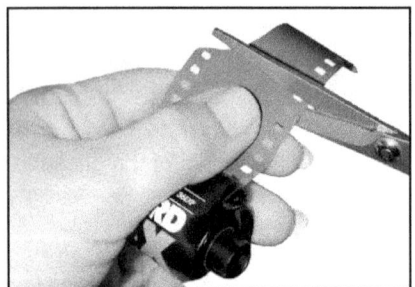

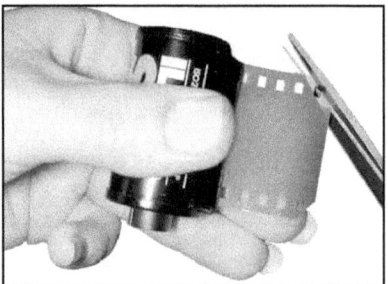

Cut the film square   Cut off the film corners

Loading a film onto a spiral reel is the most difficult part of film processing because you have to do it in complete darkness. Developing tank manufacturers have continually improved their reels over the years and most modern ones now have auto feed systems, but it's still a good idea to practice this procedure before loading your fist exposed film.

Use an old, out of date film to practice with in daylight first

Two types of reel are common - stainless steel, where you attach the film to the centre of the reel and wind outwards; or plastic, where you start the film at the outside of the reel and push or rotate it inwards. If you're going to use a stainless steel tank. Then definitely practice loading the dummy film to avoid buckling it and possibly kinking it.

A kink in the film may make the film surfaces touch which could result in uneven development. If you use a plastic reel you can gently push the film around the spiral, but again be careful of making the film buckle and try to handle it by the edges to avoid finger marks.

The reel spirals must be dry before loading the film

If they are not, you don't have a chance of loading the film. It will simply stick and will not budge. Use blotting paper and then a hair dryer to make sure all the spiral tracks are completely dry before loading any film.

Now feed the leading edge of the film into the jaws of the spiral until it is gripped under the ball bearings. I find the best approach is to push the film in at first using gentle pressure. When you can longer push it any further, continue with the rotating method This consists of rotating each of your hands alternately through about 90 degrees to feed the film gently into the spiral until you reach the cassette.

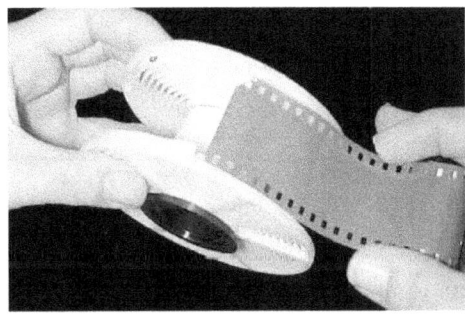

Locate film in spiral

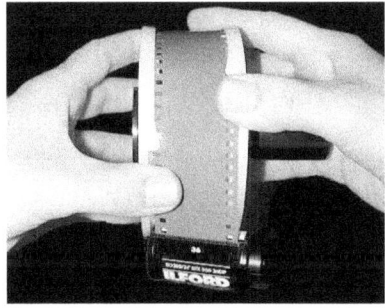

Feed the film into spiral

When you reach the end of the film cut of the end that's attached to the cassette spindle and feed the rest of the film into the spiral. Once, all the film has passed over the ball bearings it is fully loaded.

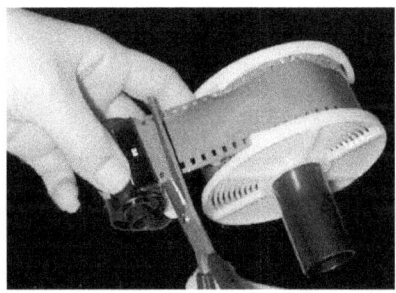

Follow the procedure that comes with your chemicals and dilute them if necessary correct processing temperature and stand the measuring cylinders in a bath of warm water to maintain their temperatures - a washing up bowl will do for this.

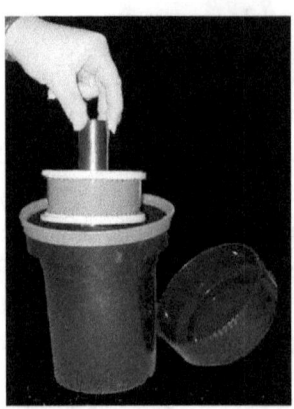

Whilst still in the dark, place the loaded film spiral reel into the developing tank and secure the top of the tank.

Once the film is loaded into the tank and the lid fitted securely, it is safe to turn on the lights.

Preparing Processing Solutions

The Pre - Development Stage

This is an optional stage but I like to first pour in some water at the development temperature to pre-warm the tank prior to development. Let the tank stand for about one minute before pouring out the water.

The Developing Stage

Get your timer ready and check the temperature of the developer. If it's at the correct temperature pour the solution into the tank. Refer to the instruction sheet with the developer for the recommended temperatures.

Now pour the developer into the tank quickly so that the whole film is covered around the same time. Switch the timer on and then tap the bottom of the tank on the palm of your hand twice to dislodge any air bubbles that may have settled on the film surface

Air bubbles can produce low-density circles on the film where the developer hasn't been able to reach the film properly.

Start the timer and use the agitation rod to turn the reel clockwise and counterclockwise in rapid movements for the first ten seconds. This further helps dislodge any remaining air bubbles.

To agitate for the rest of the development period it is best to use the inversion method where you turn the tank upside down and then back again. Do this inversion every 30 seconds.

When you are approaching the end of the development time (usually between 5 and

15 minutes depending on the developer used) get ready to pour away the developer. I usually start to pour this out about five seconds before the end time so that it's all out when the timer alarm sounds.

The Stop Bath

Now pour in the stop bath, again fast and evenly, to ensure the solution covers the film quickly and halts the development. Tap the tank on the palm of your hands as before and then agitate continuously for about 30 seconds. You can reuse stop bath several times so keep the container nearby ready to pour it back.

 Do not over use the solution though - up to three times is enough. Some stop baths have a visual indicator that changes colour when it is exhausted.

Fixing

After 30 seconds, pour out the stop bath and pour in the fixer following the recommendations in the instruction sheet that came with it.

Washing

Pour out the fixer and now wash the film. Some experts suggest that the washing stage needs to be a continuous flow of fresh water for about 30 minutes to ensure the fixer is removed.

I used to wash the film under running water for thirty minutes but in order to conserve water, I now run water through the tank for five minutes followed by filling the tank with water and replacing it six times then leaving the film to stand for about 5 minutes in fresh water. At this stage, add a drop of wetting agent to ensure the water runs off the film so that it dries without marks.

Carefully wipe the excess water off of the film with a squeegee or your fingers as described earlier and hang it up using film clips or clothes pegs. Find a suitable spot to hang the film in a dust free environment. A good hanger is the shower rail in the bathroom. Attach the top clip to that and let the film hang vertically with the weighted clip on the bottom and leave it alone to dry.

Storing your Negatives

Allow at least 45 minutes for the film to dry and then using cotton gloves, hold the film along the edges and use your scissors to cut the film into strips. Most negative sleeves hold strips of six, which are easier to handle and can be then be conveniently contact printed onto 10 x 8in paper.

File them in an album and when you make a contact print store this with the negatives for easy identification. This increases in importance as you accumulate more and more negatives. If you don't do this it can be very time consuming to find and identify individual negatives.

Darkroom Data Guide

Printing and Processing

Printing

It is assumed that the reader will already be familiar with the basic enlarging process nut here are a few tips and wrinkles that may be of use.

- Always refer to the instructions that came with your enlarger for it's operation, colour head settings and so on.

- The darkroom must be dark! Obvious I know but if your prints lack contrast it's worth checking.

- The negative or slide must always be flat in the carrier. If it isn't you may get out of focus areas on your print.

- Focus the negative on the back of an old print of the same thickness as the paper you are going to use.

- Use a focusing magnifier and adjust the focus until the grain comes into sharp focus.

- A good alternative is to get a piece of exposed film leader that has been developed and processed with a film in the normal way. Now get a pin or needle and scratch the emulsion surface to leave a ragged scratch. Put this in the negative carrier and focus the enlarger lens until the ragged edge comes into sharp focus.

- If you are production processing and want to print several prints of the same image before processing them all, use an old paper box to store them in to prevent any stray light reaching them.

- Use a good quality analyser and make sure you take the time to calibrate it properly. Record the settings for each type of film/paper/processing you use.

- Make sure you do not touch the enlarger during the exposure—this can result in a soft focus image - unless you want this effect!

- If you are near a main road as I was once, use some anti vibration pads under the enlarger baseboard to dampen the vibrations.

- Always use your analyser and exposure meter/timer in the same way. In effect, what I am saying is be *consistent*.

Print Processing

The processing of prints in the darkroom is basically the same whether you are processing black and white prints, prints from colour negatives or prints from transparencies but of course, the chemistry is different in each case.

With black and white print processing you can use a developer from one manufacturer and a fixer from another without any ill effect.

With colour print processing, however, it is best to stay with one manufacturers colour processing kit rather than mix and match chemicals from different suppliers. This is because each manufacturer matches their chemicals with each other for correct colour balance.

Mixing chemicals from different manufacturers may well result in incorrect colour balance and other problems just as it can with C41 and E6 processing so stick the kit and abide faithfully to the instructions that come with it.

However, some darkroom workers love experimenting and if this what you like - that's fine. Just be absolutely sure you faithfully, comprehensively and accurately note every step, chemical, temperature and all other variables *in this book!*

It is absolutely infuriating to achieve a stunning effect and then you are unable to produce it later. All of us fall foul of this, thinking we will remember every step but unless you have a very good memory - you won't. *You have been warned!*

As for the method you use to process your prints - this is a matter of personal preference. There are basically three methods for the average home processor:

Dish Processing

This is the traditional method, where prints are developed in open trays. There is nothing wrong with this method but there are two potential problems.

1. Colour work must be processed totally in the dark unless you buy a rather expensive special darkroom light – like the Duka type.

2. A lot of chemical solution is required - not so good if you are not processing larger quantities of prints.

Drum Processing

This is a very convenient method where the paper is placed in a light tight drum in the dark. When the lid is placed on the drum all the processing may be carried out in daylight. This method uses only small quantities of chemicals each time.

You can use the drum method with the hand agitation method just as described for film processing or you can use a Jobo type rotary drum processor.

With this system you couple the drum to a motor drive which rotates the drum. This method has the advantage of using the precisely the same conditions every time.

Deep Tank System

I am not talking about the large deep tank processors used by professional labs here but the smaller Nova type systems where prints are immersed in to vertical slots containing the solutions.

A clip is attached to the top of the print to hold it and then the print is lowered into the solution. These tanks have three or more vertical slots to contain the different chemicals required. Thus for black and white printing you would need a minimum of three slots and for colour prints you will need up to five slots depending on the process.

The print is removed from the first slot and drained before placing it in the next slot and so on until every processing stage has been completed.

Here are a few more tips and wrinkles regarding print processing:

- Make sure the paper is fully immersed in each solution and that there are no air bubbles present on the paper surface. You can see this if you are using dishes with a safelight but with the drum system, adopt the same technique for dislodging bubbles as described for film processing.

- Remove the paper from each solution five seconds before the timer rings to allow time for draining.

- If using dish processing, use a dish warmer to maintain temperature.

- Wash the prints for the recommended time as per the kit instructions. Do not skimp this stage or the prints may degrade later.

- Use a final rinse solution - some water with a drop of wetting agent in it to help prevent drying marks.

- Use a proper print squeegee to remove the surplus water. Dip the squeegee into the rinsing solution first and shake off the surplus water before applying it to the print. Alternatively use your fingers as described earlier

- Hang the print up to dry from one corner to dry naturally or you can place the prints on blotting paper if you prefer.

- If you use an electric dryer, beware of using the higher heat settings. The prints will dry faster but they will also curl badly which can be difficult to remedy. I prefer to use heat for half the drying cycle and cold air for the second which prevents this problem.

Filtration Correction Effects from Colour Transparencies

Cast in print	Required Correction	Effect in print	Effect of Overcorrection
Yellow	Add Magenta and Cyan	Less Yellow	Blue Cast
Magenta	Add Yellow and Cyan	Less Magenta	Green Cast
Red	Add Cyan	Less Red	Cyan Cast
Cyan	Add Yellow and Magenta	Less Cyan	Red Cast
Blue	Add Yellow	Less Blue	Yellow Cast
Green	Add Magenta	Less Green	Magenta Cast

Filtration Correction Effects from Colour Negatives

Cast in print	Required Correction	Effect in Print	Effect of Overcorrection
Yellow	Add Yellow	Less Yellow	Blue Cast
Magenta	Add Magenta	Less Magenta	Green Cast.
Red	Add Yellow and Magenta	Less Red	Cyan Cast
Cyan	Add Cyan	Less Cyan	Red Cast
Blue	Add Magenta and Cyan	Less Blue	Yellow Cast
Green	Add Yellow and Cyan	Less Green	Magenta Cast

Primary Colours

Red = Yellow and Magenta
Green = Yellow and Cyan
Blue = Magenta and Cyan

Elimination of Neutral Density

If all three filters are used together, an element of neutral density is formed which reduces the amount of light reaching the paper, but does nothing to change the colour of the light. It just increases the exposure time unnecessarily.

If filter adjustments are made which result in all three filters being used, then eliminate the neutral density by removing equal amounts of all three filters equal to the lowest filter value present.

Example.	Colour head is set to:	70 Y 50 M 10 C
Remove		10 Y 10 M 10 C
Result		60 Y 40 M 0 C

Darkroom Data Guide

Changing Paper Batch

Colour and paper speed may vary slightly from batch to batch. Some manufacturers provide information on the box label, which can be used to recalibrate your enlarger or your analyser. First take the filtration values used on the existing batch that gives a good result. Subtract from this the old batch values and then add the new batch values.

Example.

Existing enlarger filter values.	60 Y 50 M
Subtract old batch filter values.	50 Y 40 M
Result.	10 Y 10 M
Add new batch filter values.	5 Y 10 M
Result	15Y 20M

This gives the new basic enlarger setting to be used with the new batch of paper. If the new batch lists a different exposure/speed factor, then:

New standard exposure time = $\dfrac{\text{New batch factor}}{\text{Old batch factor}}$ x Original standard exposure time.

Filter Exposure Compensation (Kodak Values)

Each time filter values are changed, the amount of light reaching the baseboard changes, and an exposure adjustment has to be made. Use the table below to establish new exposure times.

Look up the amount that you have changed the filtration by in the table. If you have added filters, multiply your previous exposure time by the factor shown. If you subtract filters divide by the factor shown.

Filter value	Yellow	Magenta	Cyan
00	1.0	1.0	1.0
05	1.1	1.2	1.1
10	1.1	1.3	1.2
20	1.1	1.5	1.3
30	1.1	1.7	1.4
40	1.1	1.9	1.5
50	1.1	2.1	1.6

Filters added.
New exposure time = Yf x Mf x Cf x old exposure time.

Filters subtracted.
New exposure time = $\dfrac{\text{Old exposure time}}{Yf \times Mf \times Cf}$

Darkroom Data Guide

Example 2. 20 Y and 30 M added, old exposure time = 12 seconds.
New exposure time =1.1 x 1.7 x 1 x 12 = 22.5 seconds.

Example 3. 10 Y and 20 M subtracted, old exposure time = 11 seconds.
New exposure time $= \dfrac{11}{1.1 \text{ X } 1.5 \text{ X } 1} = 6.7$ seconds.

Example 4. 20 Y added and 20 M subtracted, old exposure time = 10 seconds
New exposure time = 1.1 x 10 = 11 seconds (for yellow)
which becomes $\dfrac{11}{1.5} = 7.33$ seconds (for both)

This is the same as making first a change to the yellow to give 11 seconds, and then a change to the magenta using the new value (11 seconds).

Ilford Multigrade Filters

The twelve Multigrade filters are numbered 00–5 in 1/2 steps, with the lowest filter number corresponding to the softest contrast.

Filters are available in sets of filters 8.9 x 8.9cm (31/2x31/2 inches) and 15.2 x 15.2cm (6x6 inches). They can be used above or below the lens and can be cut to fit the enlarger filter drawer. Filter sizes 30 x 30cm (11.8x11.8 inches) are available to special order.

A filter kit is available for below the lens use. The kit comprises 12 mounted contrast filters, a mounted safelight filter and a filter holder.

Multigrade filters are very easy to use: no complicated calculations are needed when changing from one filter to another. The exposure tlme for filters 00–31/2 is the same; that for filters 4–5 is double.

Multigrade filter kits are available from most good photographic darkroom materials suppliers.

When using Multigrade papers, consult your enlarger manufacturers instructions regarding the use of these filters.

Colour Head Filter Values for Ilford Multigrade Papers

The contrast of Multigrade papers can be controlled with the range of variable contrast enlarger heads that are currently available. Some of these are easier to use than others, and several give excellent results.

Many manufacturers make variable contrast heads for their enlargers, which are specially designed for use with Multigrade papers. Enlarger heads that have been designed in conjunction with Ilford include those from De Vere, Dunco, Kaiser, Leitz, LPL and Meopta.

Darkroom Data Guide

Durst	Kodak	Meopta
Dunco	Advena	Meopta
Durst	Beseler	
Kaiser	Chromega	
Kienzel	De Vere	
Leitz	Fujimoto	
Lupo	IFF	
	Jobo	
	LPL	
	Omega	
	Paterson	
	Simard	
	Vivitar	

Find the group in which your enlarger falls and read off the filter settings from the chart below. If you are using a Durst enlarger, or one that uses Durst filtration values, choose the suggested settings depending on whether the maximum magenta setting on your enlarger is 130M or 170M.

Single Filtration Values

Filter	Durst Max 170	Durst Max 130	Kodak	Meopta
00	150Y	120Y	199Y	150Y
0	90Y	70Y	90Y	90Y
½	70Y	50Y	70Y	70
1	55Y	40Y	50Y	55Y
1½	30Y	25Y	30Y	30Y
2	0	0	0	0
2½	20M	10M	5M	20M
3	45M	30M	25M	40M
3½	65M	50M	50M	65M
4	100M	75M	80M	85M
4½	140M	120M	140M	200M
5	170	130	199	-

From the table below, read off the approximate filtration needed for each contrast step. Dual filtration values usually need longer exposure times than single filtration values, but should need less adjustment to exposure times when changing contrast.

Dual Filtration Values

Filter	Durst (max 170m)	Durst (max 130m)	Kodak	Leitz Focomat V35
1	15Y/0M	120Y/0M	162Y/0M	135Y/6M
0	100Y/5M	88Y/6M	90Y/0M	105Y/12M
1/2	88Y/7M	78Y/8M	78Y/5M	77Y/11M
1	75Y/10M	64Y/12M	68Y/10M	67Y/17M
11/2	65Y/15M	53Y/17M	49Y/23M	52Y/28M
2	52Y/20M	45Y/24M	41Y/32M	39Y/43M
21/2	42Y/28M	35Y/31M	32Y/42M	32Y/51M
3	34Y/45M	24Y/42M	23Y/56M	23Y/62M
31/2	27Y/60M	17Y/53M	15Y/75M	14Y/79M
4	17Y/76M	10Y/69M	6Y/102M	10Y/95M
41/2	10Y/105M	6Y/89M	0Y/150M	15Y/154M
5	0Y/170M	0Y/130M	-	0Y/200M

Darkroom Data Guide

Equivalent Colour Head Values

Durst	Kodak/Ciba	Agfa
00	00	00
10	15	20
20	30	40
35	40	60
40	60	80
50	75	100
60	90	120
70	105	140
80	120	160
90	135	180
100	150	200
110	165	220
120	180	240
130	195	260
140	210	280
150	225	300
160	240	320
170	255	340
180	270	360
190	285	380
200	300	400

Colour Head Equivalents of Kodak cc Filters

It can sometimes be useful to imitate the effects of cc filters with the enlarger colour head. You may wish to fine-tune these to your own preferences.

Filter	Colour	Durst Y	M	C	Kodak/Ciba Y	M	C	Agfa Y	M	C
80A	Blue	00	20	60	00	30	90	00	40	120
80B	Blue	00	17	53	00	25	80	00	34	106
80C	Blue	00	11	37	00	17	55	00	22	74
80D	Blue	00	08	23	00	12	35	00	16	46
81	Yellow	03	00	00	05	00	00	06	00	00
81A	Yellow	03	01	00	05	02	00	06	02	00
81B	Yellow	07	01	00	10	02	00	14	02	00
81C	Yellow	10	03	00	15	05	00	20	06	00
81D	Yellow	17	05	00	25	07	00	34	10	00
82	Blue	00	03	07	00	05	10	00	06	14
82A	Blue	00	03	10	00	05	15	00	06	20
82B	Blue	00	05	13	00	07	20	00	10	26
82C	Blue	00	05	17	00	07	25	00	10	34
85	Orange	37	13	00	55	20	00	74	26	00
85B	Orange	43	15	00	65	22	00	86	30	00
85C	Orange	23	07	00	35	10	00	46	14	00
FL-D	Orange	40	33	00	60	50	00	80	66	00

Note. FL-D means Fluorescent to Daylight.

Darkroom Data Guide

Some Tips for Handling and Measuring Chemicals

Always treat chemicals with caution and respect.

Avoid contact with the body, particularly the eyes. Do not allow any chemicals to come into contact with your mouth.

It is advisable to wear rubber or disposable gloves to protect your hands and safety glasses. Wash your gloved hands before removing your gloves to minimize any possibility of skin contact.

Mix up chemicals in a well ventilated room to avoid breathing in fumes. Extra care is needed with fine powders to avoid breathing in airborne particles. Use a facemask if necessary.

In mixing liquid chemicals use as small a measuring cylinder as possible, which gives greater measuring accuracy.

When diluting chemicals with water, measure out the amount of chemical required first, pour into a larger measure and top up with water. This is more accurate than measuring the chemical and water separately.

If you make up solutions from powders, start with about three quarters of the final volume of water required, heated to 30 - 40 degrees Celsius (no hotter). Slowly pour the powder into the water, stirring continuously until it is completely dissolved. Then make up to the required final volume with cold water.

If you make your own solutions from your own or published formulae it can often be quite difficult weighing out the chemicals in the very small quantities required. To overcome this, it can be useful to prepare a 10% stock solution, which greatly simplifies the problem and ensures accuracy into the bargain.

To do this, dissolve 100 grammes of the chemical in about 750 ml of warm water. When the chemicals are completely dissolved, top up the solution with cold water to exactly 1 litre.

Your stock solution will now contain 1 gramme of chemical in each 10 ml of solution. If a particular formula calls for, say, 5.3 grammes of a chemical then 53 ml of the stock solution will contain this amount with much more accuracy than you can achieve by trying to weigh out 5.3 grammes (unless you have access to very accurate weighing scales).

Unfortunately, many photographic chemicals oxidize on contact with air and will deteriorate, sometimes quite rapidly. To prevent this, make sure that bottles are full and tightly stoppered. Pour the chemical into smaller bottles as it is used up or use a puff of Tetenal Protectan or similar to displace the air in the bottle.

Some photographic solutions can be quite thick, with a consistency of syrup, which makes measuring in conventional cylinders extremely difficult. To overcome this you can use a positive displacement method, for example, a hypodermic syringe body,

Cleaning Negatives

It is an unnecessary waste of time and very irritating to produce a well-exposed and balanced print that displays dust, marks, fingerprints, processing and drying marks etc.

Before starting to print, particularly if you are producing a large print it pays dividends to carefully examine the negative for such problems. It is much more difficult to retouch the print afterwards, so make sure the negative is in good condition before you print.

The best way to check a negative for such problems is to hold it, shiny side up, at an angle to a light source so that the light is reflected back from it. Keep altering the angle of the negative to the light source and you will be able to detect any blemishes.

Consult the details below for possible treatments.

Dust Marks

   1   Blow off with air
   2   Re wash film, add wetting agent to final wash, hang to dry in a dust free area.

Finger Marks

   1   Breathe on film and gently clean with lint free cloth.
   2   Use proprietary film cleaner.

Drying Marks

   1   Gently clean surface with lint free cloth and diluted Wetting agent.
   2   Re wash film as above.
   3   Use proprietary film cleaner.

Scratches

   1   Use "nose grease". Pick up some grease from the side of your nose with your finger and gently work in to the affected area with a circular motion.
   2   Use proprietary scratch remover.
   3   Coat surface of film with glycerin (this is a very messy procedure and should only be attempted as a last resort!)

Note. All the foregoing remarks apply to treatment on the ***shiny (base) side of the film***. It can be very difficult to remove blemishes from the emulsion side and it is best avoided.

If you must get rid of marks on the emulsion side then try gently with film cleaner - but test on a spare piece of film first. There is no guarantee that this will work and it is a risky procedure since you run the risk of scratching the delicate emulsion surface.

See the appendix for a list of suitable film cleaners.

Oh yes. What is this famous lint free cloth? Well a large cotton, gents handkerchief washed and boiled several times will make it soft and non fluffy and ideal as a lint free cloth - this is what I use and it's nice and cheap.

Push and Pull Processing

Push processing consists of extending the development period for a film that has been underexposed in the camera. This occurs when a film has been exposed at a higher ISO/ASA rating than that recommended by the film manufacturer. The increased development time builds up the density and effectively increases the contrast.

Pull processing consists of reducing the development period for a film that has been overexposed in the camera. This occurs when a film has been exposed at a lower ISO/ASA rating than that recommended by the film manufacturer. The reduced development time reduces the density and effectively reduces the contrast.

To "push" a film speed you would expose a film at a higher ISO/ASA rating in 1/2 or full stop increments. For example exposing a 400 ASA/ISO film at 800 ASA/ISO would be a 1-stop push. Exposing the same film at 1600 ASA/ISO represents a 2-stop push. The development time would then have to be extended to push process the film 1 stop or 2 stops to compensate.

To "pull" a film speed you would expose a film at a lower ISO/ASA rating in 1/2 or full stop increments. For example exposing a 400 ASA/ISO film at 200 ASA/ISO represents a 1-stop pull. Exposing the same film at 100 ASA/ISO represents a 2-stop pull. The development time would then have to be reduced to pull process the film 1 stop or 2 stops to compensate.

As a rule of thumb, never develop a film for less than half or more than twice the time recommended for normal development when the film is rated at its recommended speed.

Push/Pull Processing Black and White Film.

There are a large number of black and white films available from different manufacturers, which already cover the speed range 25 ASA/ISO to 3200 ASA/ISO. Many of these may be rated at other speeds.

There are also a wide variety of developers available, again, many of which may be used for push or pull processing. To list all the different combinations would be an impossible, or at least mammoth, task and could possibly constitute a book in its own right. We have, however, listed below some of the more popular films and developers available, together with notes on push and pull processing.

Please note, however, these are only suggested values and you may have to make some adjustments to these based on your own experiences and the result you are looking for. Your development technique/equipment, type of enlarger etc are all fac-

Darkroom Data Guide

tors which will influence the result.

If you have the choice of uprating a film, or buying one at the rating you require, always buy one at the correct rating. It usually gives better results.

Once you have established the result that pleases you, make a note of the details for future reference. To assist you in this we have included a set of blank tables so that you can log the information and build up your own personal data file. The tables show the development times in minutes.

Black and White Push/Pull Processing Tables

Ilford FP4 Plus							
Developer	Dilution	ISO 80	ISO 125	ISO 250			
Ilford ID11	Stock	5	6.5	8.5			
Ilford Microphen	Stock	4	5	8			
Iford Perceptol	Stock	8	10	-			
Ilford Ilfosol	1 + 9	4	4	7			
Kodak D76	Stock	5.5	6.5	8			
Kodak T-max	1 + 4	5	5.5	6			
Kodak HC110	1 + 31	5.5	6	8.5			
Agfa Rodinal	1 + 25	5	5.5	7			
FotospeedFD10	1 + 9	5	5	7			
Paterson Acutol	1 + 10	6	6	8			
Paterson Aculux	1 + 9	6.5	6.5	9			

Ilford HP5 Plus						
Developer	Dilution	ISO 200	ISO 400	ISO 800	ISO 1600	ISO 3200
Ilford ID11	Stock	5.5	7.5	10.5	14	-
Ilford Microphen	Stock	4.5	6.5	8.5	11	16
Iford Perceptol	Stock	11	15	-	-	-
Ilford Ilfosol	1 + 9	5	7	8.5	14	-
Kodak D76	Stock	5	7.5	9.5	12.5	-
Kodak T-max	1 + 4	4.5	6.5	8	9.5	11.5
Kodak HC110	1 + 31	5.5	8	11	15.5	-
Agfa Rodinal	1 + 25	4.5	6	8	-	-
FotospeedFD10	1 + 9	5.5	7	10	-	-
Paterson Acutol	1 + 10	9	9	12	-	-
Paterson Aculux	1 + 9	9	9	12	-	-

Ilford Delta 400

Developer	Dilution	ISO 200	ISO 400	ISO 800		
Ilford ID11	Stock	5	6	8		
Ilford Microphen	Stock	-	4.5	6		
Iford Perceptol	Stock	10.5	13	-		
Ilford Ilfosol	1 + 9	4	6	9		
Kodak D76	Stock	8	9	14		
Kodak T-max	1 + 4	4.5	5.5	7		
Kodak HC110	1 + 31	5	6	8		
Agfa Rodinal	1 + 25	5	6	9		
FotospeedFD10	1 + 9	5	7	10		
Paterson Acutol	1 + 10	7	8	11		
Paterson Aculux	1 + 9	9.5	11	15		

Kodak Plus X Pan

Developer	Dilution	ISO 80	ISO 125	ISO 200		
Ilford ID11	Stock	5	6.5	8.5		
Ilford Microphen	Stock	4	5.5	7.5		
Iford Perceptol	Stock	8	10	-		
Ilford Ilfosol	1 + 9	4	5	7.5		
Kodak D76	Stock	5	5.5	8		
Kodak T-max	1 + 4	5	5.5	5.5		
Kodak HC110	1 + 31	4.5	5	7		
Agfa Rodinal	1 + 25	5	5.5	7		
FotospeedFD10	1 + 9	5.5	7	8.5		
Paterson Acutol	1 + 10	7	7	9.5		
Paterson Aculux	1 + 9	6	6	8		

Kodak Tri X

Developer	Dilution	ISO 200	ISO 400	ISO 800	ISO 1600	ISO 3200
Ilford ID11	Stock	5.5	7.5	11	14.5	-
Ilford Microphen	Stock	5	6.5	9	11	15.5
Iford Perceptol	Stock	11.5	15	-	-	-
Ilford Ilfosol	1 + 9	5	7.5	8.5	14.5	-
Kodak D76	Stock	6	8	8	11.5	-
Kodak T-max	1 + 4	5	6	6	10	-
Kodak HC110	1 + 31	6.5	8	11	14	-
Agfa Rodinal	1 + 25	5	6	8	-	-
FotospeedFD10	1 + 9	7	9	12	-	-
Paterson Acutol	1 + 10	9	9	12	-	-
Paterson Aculux	1 + 9	9	9	12	-	-

Kodak T – Max 100						
Developer	Dilution	ISO 50	ISO 100	ISO 200	ISO 400	
Ilford ID11	Stock	6.5	9	9	11.5	
Ilford Microphen	Stock	6.5	8	10.5	14	
Iford Perceptol	Stock	10	13.5	-	-	
Ilford Ilfosol	1 + 9	7.5	8.5	11	15	
Kodak D76	Stock	6.5	9	9	10.5	
Kodak T-max	1 + 4	5.5	8	8	12	
Kodak HC110	1 + 31	6	7	9	11	
Agfa Rodinal	1 + 25	3	4	6	-	
FotospeedFD10	1 + 9	8	9	-	-	
Paterson Acutol	1 + 10	8	8.5	12	-	
Paterson Aculux	1 + 9	9	9	-	-	

Kodak T – Max 400						
Developer	Dilution	ISO 200	ISO 400	ISO 800	ISO1600	
Ilford ID11	Stock	6	8	11	14	
Ilford Microphen	Stock	5.5	7	9.5	13.5	
Iford Perceptol	Stock	8	10.5	-	-	
Ilford Ilfosol	1 + 9	6	7.5	9.5	13	
Kodak D76	Stock	6	8	8	10	
Kodak T-max	1 + 4	5	7	7	10	
Kodak HC110	1 + 31	4.5	6	6.5	9	
Agfa Rodinal	1 + 25	3	4	5.5	-	
FotospeedFD10	1 + 9	8.5	11	-	-	
Paterson Acutol	1 + 10	9	9.5	13	-	
Paterson Aculux	1 + 9	11	12	15	-	

All the listed development times are based on the use of a Paterson or similar developing tank using a processing temperature of 20 degrees Celsius. The tank must be agitated continuously for the first 30 seconds and then inverted and returned the right way up every 30 seconds. All times quoted are for 35mm films.

As previously stated this information is provided as a starting guide and some experimentation may be required to achieve a result that is acceptable to you. If the contrast is insufficient, increase the times. If the contrast is too high, reduce the times. This is a personal choice and these development times can be adjusted to suit your personal preferences.

There may be occasions when you want to pull or push process a film in a developer that we have not listed. If so, then the push/pull processing tables page 51 may be of help, which gives a rough starting point from which you can subsequently "fine tune" the figures, depending on the results you prefer.

Darkroom Data Guide

The term "standard" in the table means the normal development time for the film you are using, which has been exposed at the nominal ISO rating specified by the manufacturer.

Pushing a film means exposing it at a higher ISO than the film's nominal ISO rating in the camera thus underexposing it. This often used when the prevailing conditions require a higher ISO rating e.g. low light conditions or fast action shots. In general a film than has been pushed requires a longer development period to compensate.

Pulling a film means exposing it a lower ISO rating than the nominal ISO rating of the film in the camera thus overexposing it. This is often used when lighting conditions are very bright resulting in extremely fast exposure times thus limiting the effect you may be looking for. In general a film than has been pulled requires a shorter development period to compensate.

Always consult the film manufacturers information on allowable pulling and pushing. This is given in *stops*. A one-stop *push* means doubling the film speed and a one-stop *pull* means halving the film speed.

Manufacturers sometimes change the specifications of their films without notice. Most manufacturers include a data sheet which gives recommended processing times inside the film carton including pushing and pulling the film. It is always worth checking that you are using this latest information.

An alternative to shortening development time when the film is overexposed (Pull processing) is to use the normal (standard) development time as if the film had been exposed at its recommended rating. This gives a negative, which is more dense than normal and slightly more grainy, but it should be very near to normal contrast. It should print normally, but with a longer printing exposure. Use the blank tables provided to log your own results.

Darkroom Data Guide

Development Record Chart

Developer	Dilution	ISO Rating								

Darkroom Data Guide

Development Record Chart

Developer	Dilution	ISO Rating								

Darkroom Data Guide

Push/Pull Processing Table
Black and White (General)

Pull (stops)				Standard Developing Time	Push (stops)			
2.0	**1.5**	**1.0**	**0.5**		**0.5**	**1.0**	**1.5**	**2.0**
3.32	3.87	4.64	5.42	6.50	7.80	9.10	10.92	12.74
3.57	4.17	5.00	5.83	7.00	8.40	9.80	11.76	13.72
3.83	4.46	5.36	6.25	7.50	9.00	10.50	12.60	14.70
4.08	4.76	5.71	6.67	8.00	9.60	11.20	13.44	15.68
4.34	5.06	6.07	7.08	8.50	10.20	11.90	14.28	16.66
4.59	5.36	6.43	7.50	9.00	10.80	12.60	15.12	17.64
4.85	5.65	6.79	7.92	9.50	11.40	13.30	15.96	18.62
5.10	5.95	7.14	8.33	10.00	12.00	14.00	16.80	19.60
5.36	6.25	7.50	8.75	10.50	12.60	14.70	17.64	20.58
5.61	6.55	7.86	9.17	11.00	13.20	15.40	18.48	21.56
5.87	6.85	8.21	9.58	11.50	13.80	16.10	19.32	22.54
6.12	7.14	8.57	10.00	12.00	14.40	16.80	20.16	23.52
6.38	7.44	8.93	10,42	12.50	15.00	17.50	21.00	24.50
6.63	7.74	9.29	10.83	13.00	15.60	18.20	21.84	25.48
6.89	8.04	9.64	11.25	13.50	16.20	18.90	22.68	26.46
7.14	8.33	10.00	11.67	14.00	16.80	19.60	23.52	27.44

Note. It is advisable to avoid development times of less than 5 minutes where ever possible, to reduce the risk of uneven or variable results.

Darkroom Data Guide

Processing Colour Negative Film C41 Process

Processing conditions for colour films are more critical than with black and white films. If your processing is not accurate, the negative images can show a shift in colour that does not represent the original scene colours as well as it should.

As well as displaying an incorrect colour shift, incorrect processing can also affect the density and contrast of the negative.

The main areas that cause problems are:

1   Solution temperature - make sure you have an accurate thermometer. Pre-heat your tank before processing. Use a water bath to maintain temperature.

2   Solution strength - dilute the chemicals as accurately as possible. Use the smallest measuring equipment you can. Do not use a measuring cylinder that is too large where you have to estimate between two values.

3   Process time - use a stopwatch or darkroom timer if possible. Allow time for draining chemicals if the instructions call for this.

4   Agitation - Follow the recommended procedure faithfully.

Unlike black and white processing where you can choose separate chemicals (e.g. Kodak developer and Ilford fixer), most colour chemicals come as kits and it is essential to follow the manufacturers instructions to the letter.

If you do get a problem, consult the faultfinding charts for possible causes.

Processing Procedure

The development of a colour negative film often referred to as C41 film is no more complex than the processing of a black and white film.

They both require a bath of three chemicals which in this case are a Colour Developer, Stop Bath and a combined Bleach/Fixer which need to be kept at a constant temperature during the processing run.

This can been done quite simply by using a water bath i.e. a washing up dish or basin approximately 450mm x 300mm x 230mm, although size is not critical it should be able to hold enough water to be able to maintain a constant temperature.

The cooler water is simply replaced with hot water at regular intervals to maintain the temperature To begin with you need to prepare the solutions as according to the kits instructions, a word of caution however should be observed, that all mixing containers must be 100% clean as any cross contamination of any of the chemicals will result in an undesired effect on the film, therefore you must rinse all mixing/measuring containers thoroughly in clean water between the mixing of each chemical stage.

Darkroom Data Guide

There are three basic chemical solutions required to develop a colour negative film as mentioned above and the preparation of them is fairly straightforward.

Decide on a processing temperature the optimum being 38°C although you can work + or − 2°C either side providing you adjust your col our development times, the bleach/fix times remain unchanged.

Start by bringing the solutions up to your allotted processing time and load the film into the tank in complete darkness s described earlier. Beware of any neon lights from any source including instruments as they can fog films or create colour casts. Even a neon light from a power point can create an unwanted green cast.

After loading the film into the tank the next step is to process it, which takes approximately 20 minutes. The colour development and agitation times are critical to maintain constant results whilst the rinse times given in the processing guides given with each kit are a minimum recommendation, likewise the Bleach/Fix once poured can be left longer than the stated time without any adverse effects on the film.

Processing Guidelines

1. Load the film into the development tank in complete darkness

2. Ensure the chemicals are at the correct processing temperature

3. Preheat the tank and the film by adding water at 2°C higher than the processing temperature and drain after 1 minute (the water may be colored this is normal).

4. Pour in the Developer tap drum on a hard surface to release any trapped air bubbles and agitate for 20 seconds. Then agitate for 5 seconds every 30 seconds during the development time. Then drain and save the developer for re-use if possible.

5. Pour in Stop Bath and agitate for 30 seconds and drain

6. Pour in Bleach/Fix and agitate for 30 seconds and then for 5 seconds every 30 seconds, drain and save for re-use.

7. Wash in warm water for a minimum of 5 minutes or repeated changes of wa ter.

8. Rinse in warm water with a few drops of wetting agent and squeegee and hang up to dry in a warm dust free place. The film may have a whitish milky appearance as first. This is normal and will disappear when dry.

The following table describes the Photocolour II procedure which is a typical C41 process.

Darkroom Data Guide

Photo Technology

Photocolour II

Processing Stage	Time (minutes)	Processing temperature (Celsius)
Preheat	1.00	38.00
Develop	3.25	38.00
Stop bath	0.50	38.00
Bleach/Fix	6.00	38.00
Wash	5.00	30.00 to 35.00

The photocolour process allows a processing temperature from 32 to 40 degrees Celsius but for consistent results it is advisable to use the same processing temperature every time.

If you vary the processing temperature from film to film this may have to be accompanied by a similar variation in printing filtration during the enlarging stage later.

Remember– If you achieve a result you like - stick with it. Then everything else will stay the same as well - including printing filtration and print processing.

The photocolour kits (and most others) come with a comprehensive guide to processing and it pays to read it thoroughly before you start.

Darkroom Data Guide

Push and Pull Processing for Colour Negative Film C41

Most chemical kit suppliers give information on pull and push processing colour negative films and these should be consulted wherever possible.

You should note, however, that pull or push processing will not correct false colour casts that are caused by using the wrong exposure.

In particular, development modifications in excess of 1 stop should be reserved for emergency situations only.

For general guidance, adjust the development times as follows:

Exposure in Camera	Development Adjustment
Pull + 1 stop (1/2 normal ISO)	Reduce by 30%
Push - 1 stop (2 x normal ISO)	Increase by 35%
Push - 2 stops (4 x normal ISO)	Increase by 75%

The table below incorporates these values for typical development times. Times are in minutes.

Pull (stops) 1 stop	Standard Development Time	Push (stops) 1 stop	Push (stops) 2 stops
1.75	2.50	3.38	4.38
1.87	2.67	3.60	4.67
1.99	2.84	3.83	4.96
2.10	3.00	4.05	5.26
2.22	3.17	4.28	5.55
2.34	3.34	4.50	5.84
2.45	3.50	4.73	6.13
2.57	3.67	4.95	6.42
2.69	3.84	5.18	6.71
2.80	4.00	5.40	7.01
2.92	4.17	5.63	7.30
3.04	4.34	5.85	7.59
3.15	4.50	6.08	7.88
3.27	4.67	6.30	8.17
3.39	4.84	6.53	8.46
3.50	5.00	6.75	8.76
3.62	5.17	6.98	9.05
3.74	5.34	7.20	9.34
3.85	5.50	7.43	9.63
3.97	5.67	7.65	9.92
4.09	5.84	7.88	10.21
4.20	6.00	8.10	10.51

Processing Colour Slide (Transparency) Film E6 Process

The same remarks apply to processing colour slide films as for processing colour negative films.

The same care must be taken during processing to ensure accuracy of temperatures, dilutions, timing and agitation.

Again, if you encounter a problem, consult the faultfinding chart for possible causes.

There are many benefits of home processing colour slide films, although on the surface there seems to be little to recommend it. The problem is that some slide films, like Kodachrome, are sold at a price that includes processing and mounting by the manufacturers own laboratories.

Also, there are independent processing laboratories all over the country, which handle films sold without processing rights. Most of them offer a fast, reliable, high-quality service, so why do it yourself?

Benefits of home processing

As well as being satisfying, processing your own colour slide film is faster than getting it done by a professional laboratory. You can see the results within an hour of taking the pictures if you are shooting at home and have the chemicals to temperature.
This is a big advantage if you're taking studio portraits or still-life pictures, as it means you can leave your lighting in place until you see the results, make any adjustments, and re-shoot if necessary. It also enables you to shoot a test film to find out if you need any small filter adjustment on the camera to correct the colour balance before you take your pictures.

Home colour slide processing can also be cheaper but how much cheaper depends on the amount of colour slide photography you do. The more slide films you shoot, the better use of solutions you will make.

A regular processing lab charges 3.99 to process a 36-exposure film. The Tetenal Colortec E6 3 bath kit costs £25.55 and develops 12 films, which works out at £2.13 per film. You can cut the cost per film still further if you use larger kits. Kits in their largest sizes bring the cost per film down to 82 pence. If you don't have a high throughput of films, you could always share a kit with a friend.

Quality does not have to be sacrificed when you process your own colour slide films though. With care you can produce slides that are at least as good as those from professional laboratories. These labs are set up to produce commercially acceptable results from perhaps thousands of films every day.

The following tables illustrate typical E6 processing procedures fro Kodak and Photo Technology.

Darkroom Data Guide

Kodak E6

Processing Stage	Time (minutes)	Processing temperature (Celsius)
First developer	6.00	37.8
Wash	2.00	37.8
Reversal bath	2.00	37.8
Colour developer	6.00	37.8
Conditioner	2.00	37.8
Bleach	6.00	37.8
Fix	4.00	37.8
Wash	4.00	37.8
Stabilizer	0.50	37.8

Photo Technology Chrome Six

Processing Stage	Time (Minutes)	Processing temperature (Celsius)
Preheat	1.00	43.0
First developer	6.50	38.0
Wash	3.00	34.0 to 42.0
Colour developer	6.00	38.0
Wash	1.50	34.0 to 42.0
Bleach fix	10.0	34.0 to 40.0
Wash	4.00	34.0 to 42.0

The Chrome Six process also allows a wide temperature processing range from 20 to 45 degrees Celsius (but the actual processing temperature must be accurate and consistent).

An equally comprehensive guide to processing is provided with each Chrome Six kit, which you should consult in detail before processing.

Push and Pull Processing for Colour Slide (Transparency) Film

As advised for the C41 process, kit suppliers usually give information on pull and push processing which should be fully consulted before starting. As with C41, colour casts and contrast may be affected.

For general guidance adjust the first development time as follows.

Exposure in Camera	First Development Adjustment
Pull 2 stops (1/4 normal ISO)	Reduce by 50%
Pull 1 stop (1/2 normal ISO)	Reduce by 30%
Push 1 stop (2 x normal ISO)	Increase by 30%
Push 2 stops (4 x normal ISO)	Increase by 80%

Darkroom Data Guide

The table below incorporates these values for typical development times.

Pull (stops)		Standard Development Time	Push (stops)	
2 stops	1 stop		1 stop	2 stops
2.50	3.50	5.00	6.50	9.00
2.63	3.68	5.25	6.83	9.45
2.75	3.85	5.50	7.15	9.90
2.88	4.03	5.75	7.48	10.35
3.00	4.20	6.00	7.80	10.80
3.13	4.38	6.25	8.13	11.25
3.25	4.55	6.50	8.45	11.70
3.38	4.73	6.75	8.78	12.15
3.50	4.90	7.00	9.10	12.60
3.63	5.08	7.25	9.43	13.05
3.75	5.25	7.50	9.75	13.50
3.88	5.43	7.75	10.08	13.95
4.00	5.60	8.00	10.40	14.40
4.13	5.78	8.25	10.73	14.85
4.25	5.95	8.50	11.05	15.30
4.38	6.13	8.75	11.38	15.75
4.50	6.30	9.00	11.70	16.20
4.63	6.48	9.25	12.03	16.65
4.75	6.65	9.50	12.35	17.10
4.88	6.83	9.75	12.68	17.55
5.00	7.00	10.00	13.00	18.00

Darkroom Data Guide

Dilution Tables - Notes on Use

It can be difficult and fiddly, working out the quantities required to obtain a final volume which has the required dilution. To overcome this problem, three sets of dilution tables have been provided.

The first table is based on the Paterson System 4 developing tank. These tanks require a minimum of 290 ml for each 35 mm film being developed in the tank.
Thus if you want to develop one film at a dilution of 1 + 7, look down the column headed "dilution" to find "1 + 7" and then horizontally across, stopping under the set of three columns marked "1 film". In this case, under the heading C (for chemical) the required amount is 37 ml, under W (for water), the amount is 259 ml and under T (total) the amount given is the total volume you require, i.e. 296 ml.

Please note that all figures have been rounded up to a whole number to avoid quoting fractions of a ml. This will mean that total volumes may be in excess of those required, but the dilution will be accurate.

Similarly the second table is based on the Paterson System 4 tank but in this case for processing 120 size films, which require a minimum of 500 ml per film.

The third table gives dilution values for any volume that may be required in convenient 50ml intervals Once again the chemical value given has been rounded up to a whole number and frequently the total volume listed will be more than that required.

For example, suppose you require a total volume of 500 ml made up to a dilution of 1+48. The table gives C = 11 ml, W = 528 ml and T = 539 ml. This is 39 ml more than you require, so after mixing the solution simply discard 39 ml to arrive at your required volume of 500 ml.

This may sound wasteful at first glance but consider what happens if you want to achieve 500 ml exactly. The amount of chemical required would be 10.20 ml which is almost impossible to measure with the equipment in the average darkroom. The actual "wastage" of chemical in this instance would only be 0.8 ml. The rest is water.

If you wish to process a mixture of 35 mm and 120 films of the same type in the same Paterson tank, then simply add the appropriate figures together from each table.

E.g. you want to process 2 off 35 mm films and one 120 film at the same time at a dilution of 1 + 9.

From the first table (35 mm)	C = 58	W = 522	T = 580
From the second table (120)	C = 50	W = 450	T = 500
Totals required are therefore	C= 108	W = 972	T = 1080

Darkroom Data Guide

Sometimes chemicals are made up into stock solutions which have to be further diluted before use.

An example of this is Kodak's HC110 1 litre pack. In its concentrated form it has a thick, syrupy like consistency and it is almost impossible to pour this out into a measure and achieve an exact amount.

To overcome this, Kodak suggest the concentrate be diluted 1 + 3 to form a stock solution. This is further diluted 1+7 before use to give a final dilution of 1 + 31 (dilution B).

This is fine and straightforward if you are told exactly how to dilute for stock and then for use - but there are two occasions when things can become difficult.

1) If by accident you dilute the stock solution wrongly. Let us assume in the above example, you have mixed the stock solution 1+4 instead of 1 + 3 by mistake. (Yes it can happen!). The question then is what final dilution to use, since it can obviously no longer be 1 + 7.

2) If making up your own solutions from a formula, you may want to make up a stock solution for yourself.

In both these cases you will need to know how to arrive at the correct dilution figures. Fortunately, there is a simple calculation that can be made to solve these problems.

First let us look at Kodak's figures to see how they arrive at their figures.

Initial stock solution dilution = 1+3

Dilution of stock solution for use =1+7

Which gives an overall dilution of 1+31

To arrive at the correct final dilution proceed as follows.

1) Add together the (1 + 3) for the initial stock solution which gives 4.

2) Add together the overall dilution figure (1 + 31) which gives 32.

3) Divide (2) above by (1) above so $\frac{32}{4} = 8$.

4) Separate this figure (8) into two components by subtracting 1 to give in this case, 1+7.

Darkroom Data Guide

Now let assume that you have inadvertently mixed up the wrong dilution by mistake. We all do it from time to time. The question is do we throw the solution away or can we redeem the situation? Fortunately, the answer to this is yes!

Example 1.
In this example we will assume you should have made a dilution of 1 + 3 as instructed but you have used an actual dilution of 1 + 5 by mistake. This is how we correct the situation. In this case, the final working dilution required is 1 + 35.

We proceed exactly as before

Initial stock dilution   1 + 5   Add together to give 6
Required overall dilution 1 + 35   Add together to give 36

Now divide 36 by 6

$$\frac{36}{6} = 6$$

Separate into two parts to give 1 + 5, The necessary dilution to arrive at the final working dilution of 1 + 35.

Example 2.
Supposing you have made this mistake with HC110 and diluted it also at 1 + 5 instead of 1 + 3 for your stock solution. If we had used the correct stock dilution of 1 + 3. we would normally need to further dilute it 1 + 7 to give the correct working dilution of 1 + 31. In this case, proceeding as before:

Initial stock dilution   1 + 5   Add together to give 6
Required overall dilution 1 + 31   Add together to give 33

Now divide 36 by 6

$$\frac{32}{6} = 5.33$$

Separate into two parts to give 1 + 4.33!! Oh dear what do we do now? We can't dilute using these figures! What we have to do is to convert the awkward figure into a whole number—like this. If we multiply 4.33 by 3 we get the number 13. So we multiply both figures by 3 to maintain the same ratio. So we arrive at a dilution of 3 + 13.

Don't forget you can use the dilution tables provided to assist you in making up any quantity of stock or working solution you require.

It is good practice to record all information regarding initial, working and final dilutions for future reference and blank table have been provided for you to do just this with your own data and results. An example based on HC110 has been included.

Don't skip this recording of your data. *You will never remember it later!*

Darkroom Data Guide

Dilution Tables for Paterson Developing Tanks
Based on 290 ml per film (35mm)

Dilution			1 Film			2 Films			3 Films			4 Films			5 Films		
			C	W	T	C	W	T	C	W	T	C	W	T	C	W	T
1	+	1	145	145	290	290	290	580	435	435	870	580	580	1160	725	725	1450
1	+	2	97	194	291	194	388	582	290	580	870	387	774	1161	484	968	1452
1	+	3	73	219	292	145	435	580	218	654	872	290	870	1160	363	1089	1452
1	+	4	58	232	290	116	464	580	174	696	870	232	928	1160	290	1160	1450
1	+	5	49	245	294	97	485	582	145	725	870	194	970	1164	242	1210	1452
1	+	6	42	252	294	83	498	581	125	750	875	166	996	1162	208	1248	1456
1	+	7	37	259	296	73	511	584	109	763	872	145	1015	1160	182	1274	1456
1	+	8	33	264	297	65	520	585	97	776	873	129	1032	1161	162	1296	1458
1	+	9	29	261	290	58	522	580	87	783	870	116	1044	1160	145	1305	1450
1	+	10	27	270	297	53	530	583	80	800	880	106	1060	1166	132	1320	1452
1	+	11	25	275	300	49	539	588	73	803	876	97	1067	1164	121	1331	1452
1	+	12	23	276	299	45	540	585	67	804	871	90	1080	1170	112	1344	1456
1	+	13	21	273	294	42	546	588	63	819	882	83	1079	1162	104	1352	1456
1	+	14	20	280	300	39	546	585	58	812	870	78	1092	1170	97	1358	1455
1	+	15	19	285	304	37	555	592	55	825	880	73	1095	1168	91	1365	1456
1	+	16	18	288	306	35	560	595	52	832	884	69	1104	1173	86	1376	1462
1	+	17	17	289	306	33	561	594	49	833	882	65	1105	1170	81	1377	1458
1	+	18	16	288	304	31	558	589	46	828	874	62	1116	1178	77	1386	1463
1	+	19	15	285	300	29	551	580	44	836	880	58	1102	1160	73	1387	1460
1	+	20	14	280	294	28	560	588	42	840	882	56	1120	1176	70	1400	1470
1	+	21	14	294	308	27	567	594	40	840	880	53	1113	1166	66	1386	1452
1	+	22	13	286	299	26	572	598	38	836	874	51	1122	1173	64	1408	1472
1	+	23	13	299	312	25	575	600	37	851	888	49	1127	1176	61	1403	1464
1	+	24	12	288	300	24	576	600	35	840	875	47	1128	1175	58	1392	1450
1	+	25	12	300	312	23	575	598	34	850	884	45	1125	1170	56	1400	1456
1	+	26	11	286	297	22	572	594	33	858	891	43	1118	1161	54	1404	1458
1	+	27	11	297	308	21	567	588	32	864	896	42	1134	1176	52	1404	1456
1	+	28	10	280	290	20	560	580	30	840	870	40	1120	1160	50	1400	1450
1	+	29	10	290	300	20	580	600	29	841	870	39	1131	1170	49	1421	1470
1	+	30	10	300	310	19	570	589	29	870	899	38	1140	1178	47	1410	1457
1	+	31	10	310	320	19	589	608	28	868	896	37	1147	1184	46	1426	1472
1	+	32	9	288	297	18	576	594	27	864	891	36	1152	1188	44	1408	1452
1	+	33	9	297	306	18	594	612	26	858	884	35	1155	1190	43	1419	1462
1	+	34	9	306	315	17	578	595	25	850	875	34	1156	1190	42	1428	1470
1	+	35	9	315	324	17	595	612	25	875	900	33	1155	1188	41	1435	1476
1	+	36	8	288	296	16	576	592	24	864	888	32	1152	1184	40	1440	1480
1	+	37	8	296	304	16	592	608	23	851	874	31	1147	1178	39	1443	1482
1	+	38	8	304	312	15	570	585	23	874	897	30	1140	1170	38	1444	1482
1	+	39	8	312	320	15	585	600	22	858	880	29	1131	1160	37	1443	1480
1	+	40	8	320	328	15	600	615	22	880	902	29	1160	1189	36	1440	1476
1	+	41	7	287	294	14	574	588	21	861	882	28	1148	1176	35	1435	1470
1	+	42	7	294	301	14	588	602	21	882	903	27	1134	1161	34	1428	1462
1	+	43	7	301	308	14	602	616	20	860	880	27	1161	1188	33	1419	1452
1	+	44	7	308	315	13	572	585	20	880	900	26	1144	1170	33	1452	1485
1	+	45	7	315	322	13	585	598	19	855	874	26	1170	1196	32	1440	1472
1	+	46	7	322	329	13	598	611	19	874	893	25	1150	1175	31	1426	1457
1	+	47	7	329	336	13	611	624	19	893	912	25	1175	1200	31	1457	1488
1	+	48	6	288	294	12	576	588	18	864	882	24	1152	1176	30	1440	1470
1	+	49	6	294	300	12	588	600	18	882	900	24	1176	1200	29	1421	1450
1	+	50	6	300	306	12	600	612	18	900	918	23	1150	1173	29	1450	1479

Dilution Tables for Paterson Developing Tanks
Based on 500 ml per film (120)

Dilution			1 Film			2 Films			3 Films			4 Films			5 Films		
			C	W	T	C	W	T	C	W	T	C	W	T	C	W	T
1	+	1	250	250	500	500	500	1000	750	750	1500	1000	1000	2000	1250	1250	2500
1	+	2	167	334	501	334	668	1002	500	1000	1500	667	1334	2001	834	1668	2502
1	+	3	125	375	500	250	750	1000	375	1125	1500	500	1500	2000	625	1875	2500
1	+	4	100	400	500	200	800	1000	300	1200	1500	400	1600	2000	500	2000	2500
1	+	5	84	420	504	167	835	1002	250	1250	1500	334	1670	2004	417	2085	2502
1	+	6	72	432	504	143	858	1001	215	1290	1505	286	1716	2002	358	2148	2506
1	+	7	63	441	504	125	875	1000	188	1316	1504	250	1750	2000	313	2191	2504
1	+	8	56	448	504	112	896	1008	167	1336	1503	223	1784	2007	278	2224	2502
1	+	9	50	450	500	100	900	1000	150	1350	1500	200	1800	2000	250	2250	2500
1	+	10	46	460	506	91	910	1001	137	1370	1507	182	1820	2002	228	2280	2508
1	+	11	42	462	504	84	924	1008	125	1375	1500	167	1837	2004	209	2299	2508
1	+	12	39	468	507	77	924	1001	116	1392	1508	154	1848	2002	193	2316	2509
1	+	13	36	468	504	72	936	1008	108	1404	1512	143	1859	2002	179	2327	2506
1	+	14	34	476	510	67	938	1005	100	1400	1500	134	1876	2010	167	2338	2505
1	+	15	32	480	512	63	945	1008	94	1410	1504	125	1875	2000	157	2355	2512
1	+	16	30	480	510	59	944	1003	89	1424	1513	118	1888	2006	148	2368	2516
1	+	17	28	476	504	56	952	1008	84	1428	1512	112	1904	2016	139	2363	2502
1	+	18	27	486	513	53	954	1007	79	1422	1501	106	1908	2014	132	2376	2508
1	+	19	25	475	500	50	950	1000	75	1425	1500	100	1900	2000	125	2375	2500
1	+	20	24	480	504	48	960	1008	72	1440	1512	96	1920	2016	120	2400	2520
1	+	21	23	483	506	46	966	1012	69	1449	1518	91	1911	2002	114	2394	2508
1	+	22	22	484	506	44	968	1012	66	1452	1518	87	1914	2001	109	2398	2507
1	+	23	21	483	504	42	966	1008	63	1449	1512	84	1932	2016	105	2415	2520
1	+	24	20	480	500	40	960	1000	60	1440	1500	80	1920	2000	100	2400	2500
1	+	25	20	500	520	39	975	1014	58	1450	1508	77	1925	2002	97	2425	2522
1	+	26	19	494	513	38	988	1026	56	1456	1512	75	1950	2025	93	2418	2511
1	+	27	18	486	504	36	972	1008	54	1458	1512	72	1944	2016	90	2430	2520
1	+	28	18	504	522	35	980	1015	52	1456	1508	69	1932	2001	87	2436	2523
1	+	29	17	493	510	34	986	1020	50	1450	1500	67	1943	2010	84	2436	2520
1	+	30	17	510	527	33	990	1023	49	1470	1519	65	1950	2015	81	2430	2511
1	+	31	16	496	512	32	992	1024	47	1457	1504	63	1953	2016	79	2449	2528
1	+	32	16	512	528	31	992	1023	46	1472	1518	61	1952	2013	76	2432	2508
1	+	33	15	495	510	30	990	1020	45	1485	1530	59	1947	2006	74	2442	2516
1	+	34	15	510	525	29	986	1015	43	1462	1505	58	1972	2030	72	2448	2520
1	+	35	14	490	504	28	980	1008	42	1470	1512	56	1960	2016	70	2450	2520
1	+	36	14	504	518	28	1008	1036	41	1476	1517	55	1980	2035	68	2448	2516
1	+	37	14	518	532	27	999	1026	40	1480	1520	53	1961	2014	66	2442	2508
1	+	38	13	494	507	26	988	1014	39	1482	1521	52	1976	2028	65	2470	2535
1	+	39	13	507	520	25	975	1000	38	1482	1520	50	1950	2000	63	2457	2520
1	+	40	13	520	533	25	1000	1025	37	1480	1517	49	1960	2009	61	2440	2501
1	+	41	12	492	504	24	984	1008	36	1476	1512	48	1968	2016	60	2460	2520
1	+	42	12	504	516	24	1008	1032	35	1470	1505	47	1974	2021	59	2478	2537
1	+	43	12	516	528	23	989	1012	35	1505	1540	46	1978	2024	57	2451	2508
1	+	44	12	528	540	23	1012	1035	34	1496	1530	45	1980	2025	56	2464	2520
1	+	45	11	495	506	22	990	1012	33	1485	1518	44	1980	2024	55	2475	2530
1	+	46	11	506	517	22	1012	1034	32	1472	1504	43	1978	2021	54	2484	2538
1	+	47	11	517	528	21	987	1008	32	1504	1536	42	1974	2016	53	2491	2544
1	+	48	11	528	539	21	1008	1029	31	1488	1519	41	1968	2009	52	2496	2548
1	+	49	10	490	500	20	980	1000	30	1470	1500	40	1960	2000	50	2450	2500
1	+	50	10	500	510	20	1000	1020	30	1500	1530	40	2000	2040	50	2500	2550

Darkroom Data Guide

Dilution Tables—General

Dilution			100 ml			250 ml			500 ml			750 ml			1000 ml		
			C	W	T	C	W	T	C	W	T	C	W	T	C	W	T
1	+	1	50	50	100	125	125	250	250	250	500	375	375	750	500	500	1000
1	+	2	34	68	102	84	168	252	167	334	501	250	500	750	334	668	1002
1	+	3	25	75	100	63	189	252	125	375	500	188	564	752	250	750	1000
1	+	4	20	80	100	50	200	250	100	400	500	150	600	750	200	800	1000
1	+	5	17	85	102	42	210	252	84	420	504	125	625	750	167	835	1002
1	+	6	15	90	105	36	216	252	72	432	504	108	648	756	143	858	1001
1	+	7	13	91	104	32	224	256	63	441	504	94	658	752	125	875	1000
1	+	8	12	96	108	28	224	252	56	448	504	84	672	756	112	896	1008
1	+	9	10	90	100	25	225	250	50	450	500	75	675	750	100	900	1000
1	+	10	10	100	110	23	230	253	46	460	506	69	690	759	91	910	1001
1	+	11	9	99	108	21	231	252	42	462	504	63	693	756	84	924	1008
1	+	12	8	96	104	20	240	260	39	468	507	58	696	754	77	924	1001
1	+	13	8	104	112	18	234	252	36	468	504	54	702	756	72	936	1008
1	+	14	7	98	105	17	238	255	34	476	510	50	700	750	67	938	1005
1	+	15	7	105	112	16	240	256	32	480	512	47	705	752	63	945	1008
1	+	16	6	96	102	15	240	255	30	480	510	45	720	765	59	944	1003
1	+	17	6	102	108	14	238	252	28	476	504	42	714	756	56	952	1008
1	+	18	6	108	114	14	252	266	27	486	513	40	720	760	53	954	1007
1	+	19	5	95	100	13	247	260	25	475	500	38	722	760	50	950	1000
1	+	20	5	100	105	12	240	252	24	480	504	36	720	756	48	960	1008
1	+	21	5	105	110	12	252	264	23	483	506	35	735	770	46	966	1012
1	+	22	5	110	115	11	242	253	22	484	506	33	726	759	44	968	1012
1	+	23	5	115	120	11	253	264	21	483	504	32	736	768	42	966	1008
1	+	24	4	96	100	10	240	250	20	480	500	30	720	750	40	960	1000
1	+	25	4	100	104	10	250	260	20	500	520	29	725	754	39	975	1014
1	+	26	4	104	108	10	260	270	19	494	513	28	728	756	38	988	1026
1	+	27	4	108	112	9	243	252	18	486	504	27	729	756	36	972	1008
1	+	28	4	112	116	9	252	261	18	504	522	26	728	754	35	980	1015
1	+	29	4	116	120	9	261	270	17	493	510	25	725	750	34	986	1020
1	+	30	4	120	124	9	270	279	17	510	527	25	750	775	33	990	1023
1	+	31	4	124	128	8	248	256	16	496	512	24	744	768	32	992	1024
1	+	32	4	128	132	8	256	264	16	512	528	23	736	759	31	992	1023
1	+	33	3	99	102	8	264	272	15	495	510	23	759	782	30	990	1020
1	+	34	3	102	105	8	272	280	15	510	525	22	748	770	29	986	1015
1	+	35	3	105	108	7	245	252	14	490	504	21	735	756	28	980	1008
1	+	36	3	108	111	7	252	259	14	504	518	21	756	777	28	1008	1036
1	+	37	3	111	114	7	259	266	14	518	532	20	740	760	27	999	1026
1	+	38	3	114	117	7	266	273	13	494	507	20	760	780	26	988	1014
1	+	39	3	117	120	7	273	280	13	507	520	19	741	760	25	975	1000
1	+	40	3	120	123	7	280	287	13	520	533	19	760	779	25	1000	1025
1	+	41	3	123	126	6	246	252	12	492	504	18	738	756	24	984	1008
1	+	42	3	126	129	6	252	258	12	504	516	18	756	774	24	1008	1032
1	+	43	3	129	132	6	258	264	12	516	528	18	774	792	23	989	1012
1	+	44	3	132	135	6	264	270	12	528	540	17	748	765	23	1012	1035
1	+	45	3	135	138	6	270	276	11	495	506	17	765	782	22	990	1012
1	+	46	3	138	141	6	276	282	11	506	517	16	736	752	22	1012	1034
1	+	47	3	141	144	6	282	288	11	517	528	16	752	768	21	987	1008
1	+	48	3	144	147	6	288	294	11	528	539	16	768	784	21	1008	1029
1	+	49	2	98	100	5	245	250	10	490	500	15	735	750	20	980	1000
1	+	50	2	100	102	5	250	255	10	500	510	15	750	765	20	1000	1020

42

Darkroom Data Guide

Dilution Tables—General

Dilution			1250 ml			1500 ml			1750 ml			2000 ml			2250 ml		
			C	W	T	C	W	T	C	W	T	C	W	T	C	W	T
1	+	1	625	625	1250	750	750	1500	875	875	1750	1000	1000	2000	1125	1125	2250
1	+	2	417	834	1251	500	1000	1500	584	1168	1752	667	1334	2001	750	1500	2250
1	+	3	313	939	1252	375	1125	1500	438	1314	1752	500	1500	2000	563	1689	2252
1	+	4	250	1000	1250	300	1200	1500	350	1400	1750	400	1600	2000	450	1800	2250
1	+	5	209	1045	1254	250	1250	1500	292	1460	1752	334	1670	2004	375	1875	2250
1	+	6	179	1074	1253	215	1290	1505	250	1500	1750	286	1716	2002	322	1932	2254
1	+	7	157	1099	1256	188	1316	1504	219	1533	1752	250	1750	2000	282	1974	2256
1	+	8	139	1112	1251	167	1336	1503	195	1560	1755	223	1784	2007	250	2000	2250
1	+	9	125	1125	1250	150	1350	1500	175	1575	1750	200	1800	2000	225	2025	2250
1	+	10	114	1140	1254	137	1370	1507	160	1600	1760	182	1820	2002	205	2050	2255
1	+	11	105	1155	1260	125	1375	1500	146	1606	1752	167	1837	2004	188	2068	2256
1	+	12	97	1164	1261	116	1392	1508	135	1620	1755	154	1848	2002	174	2088	2262
1	+	13	90	1170	1260	108	1404	1512	125	1625	1750	143	1859	2002	161	2093	2254
1	+	14	84	1176	1260	100	1400	1500	117	1638	1755	134	1876	2010	150	2100	2250
1	+	15	79	1185	1264	94	1410	1504	110	1650	1760	125	1875	2000	141	2115	2256
1	+	16	74	1184	1258	89	1424	1513	103	1648	1751	118	1888	2006	133	2128	2261
1	+	17	70	1190	1260	84	1428	1512	98	1666	1764	112	1904	2016	125	2125	2250
1	+	18	66	1188	1254	79	1422	1501	93	1674	1767	106	1908	2014	119	2142	2261
1	+	19	63	1197	1260	75	1425	1500	88	1672	1760	100	1900	2000	113	2147	2260
1	+	20	60	1200	1260	72	1440	1512	84	1680	1764	96	1920	2016	108	2160	2268
1	+	21	57	1197	1254	69	1449	1518	80	1680	1760	91	1911	2002	103	2163	2266
1	+	22	55	1210	1265	66	1452	1518	77	1694	1771	87	1914	2001	98	2156	2254
1	+	23	53	1219	1272	63	1449	1512	73	1679	1752	84	1932	2016	94	2162	2256
1	+	24	50	1200	1250	60	1440	1500	70	1680	1750	80	1920	2000	90	2160	2250
1	+	25	49	1225	1274	58	1450	1508	68	1700	1768	77	1925	2002	87	2175	2262
1	+	26	47	1222	1269	56	1456	1512	65	1690	1755	75	1950	2025	84	2184	2268
1	+	27	45	1215	1260	54	1458	1512	63	1701	1764	72	1944	2016	81	2187	2268
1	+	28	44	1232	1276	52	1456	1508	61	1708	1769	69	1932	2001	78	2184	2262
1	+	29	42	1218	1260	50	1450	1500	59	1711	1770	67	1943	2010	75	2175	2250
1	+	30	41	1230	1271	49	1470	1519	57	1710	1767	65	1950	2015	73	2190	2263
1	+	31	40	1240	1280	47	1457	1504	55	1705	1760	63	1953	2016	71	2201	2272
1	+	32	38	1216	1254	46	1472	1518	54	1728	1702	61	1952	2013	69	2208	2277
1	+	33	37	1221	1258	45	1485	1530	52	1716	1768	59	1947	2006	67	2211	2278
1	+	34	36	1224	1260	43	1462	1505	50	1700	1750	58	1972	2030	65	2210	2275
1	+	35	35	1225	1260	42	1470	1512	49	1715	1764	56	1960	2016	63	2205	2268
1	+	36	34	1224	1258	41	1476	1517	48	1728	1776	55	1980	2035	61	2196	2257
1	+	37	33	1221	1254	40	1480	1520	47	1739	1786	53	1961	2014	60	2220	2280
1	+	38	33	1254	1287	39	1482	1521	45	1710	1755	52	1976	2028	58	2204	2262
1	+	39	32	1248	1280	38	1482	1520	44	1716	1760	50	1950	2000	57	2223	2280
1	+	40	31	1240	1271	37	1480	1517	43	1720	1763	49	1960	2009	55	2200	2255
1	+	41	30	1230	1260	36	1476	1512	42	1722	1764	48	1968	2016	54	2214	2268
1	+	42	30	1260	1290	35	1470	1505	41	1722	1763	47	1974	2021	53	2226	2279
1	+	43	29	1247	1276	35	1505	1540	40	1720	1760	46	1978	2024	52	2236	2288
1	+	44	28	1232	1260	34	1496	1530	39	1716	1755	45	1980	2025	50	2200	2250
1	+	45	28	1260	1288	33	1485	1518	39	1755	1794	44	1980	2024	49	2205	2254
1	+	46	27	1242	1269	32	1472	1504	38	1748	1786	43	1978	2021	48	2208	2256
1	+	47	27	1269	1296	32	1504	1536	37	1739	1776	42	1974	2016	47	2209	2256
1	+	48	26	1248	1274	31	1488	1519	36	1728	1764	41	1968	2009	46	2208	2254
1	+	49	25	1225	1250	30	1470	1500	35	1715	1750	40	1960	2000	45	2205	2250
1	+	50	25	1250	1275	30	1500	1530	35	1750	1785	40	2000	2040	45	2250	2295

Dilution Tables—General

Dilution		2500 ml C	W	T	3000 ml C	W	T	3500 ml C	W	T	4000 ml C	W	T	5000 ml C	W	T
1 + 1		1250	1250	2500	1500	1500	3000	1750	1750	3500	2000	2000	4000	2500	2500	5000
1 + 2		834	1668	2502	1000	2000	3000	1167	2334	3501	1334	2668	4002	1667	3334	5001
1 + 3		625	1875	2500	750	2250	3000	875	2625	3500	1000	3000	4000	1250	3750	5000
1 + 4		500	2000	2500	600	2400	3000	700	2800	3500	800	3200	4000	1000	4000	5000
1 + 5		417	2085	2502	500	2500	3000	584	2920	3504	667	3335	4002	834	4170	5004
1 + 6		358	2148	2506	429	2574	3003	500	3000	3500	572	3432	4004	715	4290	5005
1 + 7		313	2191	2504	375	2625	3000	438	3066	3504	500	3500	4000	625	4375	5000
1 + 8		278	2224	2502	334	2672	3006	389	3112	3501	445	3560	4005	556	4448	5004
1 + 9		250	2250	2500	300	2700	3000	350	3150	3500	400	3600	4000	500	4500	5000
1 + 10		228	2280	2508	273	2730	3003	319	3190	3509	364	3640	4004	455	4550	5005
1 + 11		209	2299	2508	250	2750	3000	292	3212	3504	334	3674	4008	417	4587	5004
1 + 12		193	2316	2509	231	2772	3003	270	3240	3510	308	3696	4004	385	4620	5005
1 + 13		179	2327	2506	215	2795	3010	250	3250	3500	286	3718	4004	358	4654	5012
1 + 14		167	2338	2505	200	2800	3000	234	3276	3510	267	3738	4005	334	4676	5010
1 + 15		157	2355	2512	188	2820	3008	219	3285	3504	250	3750	4000	313	4695	5008
1 + 16		148	2368	2516	177	2832	3009	206	3296	3502	236	3776	4012	295	4720	5015
1 + 17		139	2363	2502	167	2839	3006	195	3315	3510	223	3791	4014	278	4726	5004
1 + 18		132	2376	2508	158	2844	3002	185	3330	3515	211	3798	4009	264	4752	5016
1 + 19		125	2375	2500	150	2850	3000	175	3325	3500	200	3800	4000	250	4750	5000
1 + 20		120	2400	2520	143	2860	3003	167	3340	3507	191	3820	4011	239	4780	5019
1 + 21		114	2394	2508	137	2877	3014	160	3360	3520	182	3822	4004	228	4788	5016
1 + 22		109	2398	2507	131	2882	3013	153	3366	3519	174	3828	4002	218	4796	5014
1 + 23		105	2415	2520	125	2875	3000	146	3358	3504	167	3841	4008	209	4807	5016
1 + 24		100	2400	2500	120	2880	3000	140	3360	3500	160	3840	4000	200	4800	5000
1 + 25		97	2425	2522	116	2900	3016	135	3375	3510	154	3850	4004	193	4825	5018
1 + 26		93	2418	2511	112	2912	3024	130	3380	3510	149	3874	4023	186	4836	5022
1 + 27		90	2430	2520	108	2916	3024	125	3375	3500	143	3861	4004	179	4833	5012
1 + 28		87	2436	2523	104	2912	3016	121	3388	3509	138	3864	4002	173	4844	5017
1 + 29		84	2436	2520	100	2900	3000	117	3393	3510	134	3886	4020	167	4843	5010
1 + 30		81	2430	2511	97	2910	3007	113	3390	3503	130	3900	4030	162	4860	5022
1 + 31		79	2449	2528	94	2914	3008	110	3410	3520	125	3875	4000	157	4867	5024
1 + 32		76	2432	2508	91	2912	3003	107	3424	3531	122	3904	4026	152	4864	5016
1 + 33		74	2442	2516	89	2937	3026	103	3399	3502	118	3894	4012	148	4884	5032
1 + 34		72	2448	2520	86	2924	3010	100	3400	3500	115	3910	4025	143	4862	5005
1 + 35		70	2450	2520	84	2940	3024	98	3430	3528	112	3920	4032	139	4865	5004
1 + 36		68	2448	2516	82	2952	3034	95	3420	3515	109	3924	4033	136	4896	5032
1 + 37		66	2442	2508	79	2923	3002	93	3441	3534	106	3922	4028	132	4884	5016
1 + 38		65	2470	2535	77	2926	3003	90	3420	3510	103	3914	4017	129	4902	5031
1 + 39		63	2457	2520	75	2925	3000	88	3432	3520	100	3900	4000	125	4875	5000
1 + 40		61	2440	2501	74	2960	3034	86	3440	3526	98	3920	4018	122	4880	5002
1 + 41		60	2460	2520	72	2952	3024	84	3444	3528	96	3936	4032	120	4920	5040
1 + 42		59	2478	2537	70	2940	3010	82	3444	3526	94	3948	4042	117	4914	5031
1 + 43		57	2451	2508	69	2967	3036	80	3440	3520	91	3913	4004	114	4902	5016
1 + 44		56	2464	2520	67	2948	3015	78	3432	3510	89	3916	4005	112	4928	5040
1 + 45		55	2475	2530	66	2970	3036	77	3465	3542	87	3915	4002	109	4905	5014
1 + 46		54	2484	2538	64	2944	3008	75	3450	3525	86	3956	4042	107	4922	5029
1 + 47		53	2491	2544	63	2961	3024	73	3431	3504	84	3948	4032	105	4935	5040
1 + 48		52	2496	2548	62	2976	3038	72	3456	3528	82	3936	4018	103	4944	5047
1 + 49		50	2450	2500	60	2940	3000	70	3430	3500	80	3920	4000	100	4900	5000
1 + 50		50	2500	2550	59	2950	3009	69	3450	3519	79	3950	4029	99	4950	5049

Darkroom Data Guide

Exposure Compensation

After having made a print, you may decide it is too light or too dark and wish to produce another one with the correct exposure.

The correct and easiest way to do this is to try and decide on how many stops you wish to later the exposure by – just as you would do with your camera. It is easy to alter exposures in full stops by using the click stops on the enlarger lens. Each click stop either halves or doubles the exposure – just as with your camera.

If, however, you want to change the exposure by say, 1/3 stop, it is not so easy. For example, if a print is made with an exposure of 10 seconds, a 1/3 stop increase is not 13.33 seconds as you might expect but 12.57 seconds.

This is why I have provided exposure compensation tables – to make this process easy.

Example 1

The test print exposure is 15 seconds and 0.5 stop increase is required.

Look down the left hand column headed "First Exposure" until you reach 15. Now look across the table under the heading "0.5". Where the row and column intersect, the new exposure can be found as 21.21 seconds.

Example 2

The test print exposure is 12 seconds and 1/3 (- 0.33) stop decrease is required.

As before, Look down the left hand column headed "First Exposure" until you reach 12. Now look across the table under the heading "0.33". Where the row and column intersect, the new exposure can be found as 9.95 seconds.

Please note that reductions in exposures are shown as negative (e.g. – 0.33)

Darkroom Data Guide

Exposure Compensation Tables

First Exposure secs	-0.75	-0.66	-0.50	-0.33	-0.25	0.25	0.33	0.50	0.66	0.75
1	0.60	0.64	0.71	0.80	0.85	1.19	1.26	1.42	1.59	1.69
2	1.19	1.27	1.42	1.60	1.69	2.38	2.52	2.83	3.17	3.37
3	1.79	1.90	2.13	2.39	2.53	3.57	3.78	4.25	4.75	5.05
4	2.38	2.54	2.83	3.19	3.37	4.76	5.03	5.66	6.33	6.73
5	2.98	3.17	3.54	3.98	4.21	5.95	6.29	7.08	7.91	8.41
6	3.57	3.80	4.25	4.78	5.05	7.14	7.55	8.49	9.49	10.10
7	4.17	4.44	4.95	5.57	5.89	8.33	8.80	9.90	11.07	11.78
8	4.76	5.07	5.66	6.37	6.73	9.52	10.06	11.32	12.65	13.46
9	5.36	5.70	6.37	7.16	7.57	10.71	11.32	12.73	14.23	15.14
10	5.95	6.33	7.08	7.96	8.41	11.90	12.58	14.15	15.81	16.82
11	6.55	6.97	7.78	8.76	9.25	13.09	13.83	15.56	17.39	18.50
12	7.14	7.60	8.49	9.55	10.10	14.28	15.09	16.98	18.97	20.19
13	7.73	8.23	9.20	10.35	10.94	15.46	16.35	18.39	20.55	21.87
14	8.33	8.87	9.90	11.14	11.78	16.65	17.60	19.80	22.13	23.55
15	8.92	9.50	10.61	11.94	12.62	17.84	18.86	21.22	23.71	25.23
16	9.52	10.13	11.32	12.73	13.46	19.03	20.12	22.63	25.29	26.91
17	10.11	10.76	12.03	13.53	14.30	20.22	21.37	24.05	26.87	28.60
18	10.71	11.40	12.73	14.32	15.14	21.41	22.63	25.46	28.45	30.28
19	11.30	12.03	13.44	15.12	15.98	22.60	23.89	26.88	30.03	31.96
20	11.90	12.66	14.15	15.92	16.82	23.79	25.15	28.29	31.61	33.64
21	12.49	13.30	14.85	16.71	17.66	24.98	26.40	29.70	33.19	35.32
22	13.09	13.93	15.56	17.51	18.50	26.17	27.66	31.12	34.77	37.00
23	13.68	14.56	16.27	18.30	19.35	27.36	28.92	32.53	36.35	38.69
24	14.28	15.19	16.98	19.10	20.19	28.55	30.17	33.95	37.93	40.37
25	14.87	15.83	17.68	19.89	21.03	29.74	31.43	35.36	39.51	42.05
26	15.46	16.46	18.39	20.69	21.87	30.92	32.69	36.77	41.09	43.73
27	16.06	17.09	19.10	21.48	22.71	32.11	33.94	38.19	42.67	45.41
28	16.65	17.73	19.80	22.28	23.55	33.30	35.20	39.60	44.25	47.10
29	17.25	18.36	20.51	23.08	24.39	34.49	36.46	41.02	45.83	48.78
30	17.84	18.99	21.22	23.87	25.23	35.68	37.72	42.43	47.41	50.46
31	18.44	19.62	21.93	24.67	26.07	36.87	38.97	43.85	48.99	52.14
32	19.03	20.26	22.63	25.46	26.91	38.06	40.23	45.26	50.57	53.82
33	19.63	20.89	23.34	26.26	27.75	39.25	41.49	46.67	52.15	55.50
34	20.22	21.52	24.05	27.05	28.60	40.44	42.74	48.09	53.73	57.19
35	20.82	22.16	24.75	27.85	29.44	41.63	44.00	49.50	55.31	58.87
36	21.41	22.79	25.46	28.64	30.28	42.82	45.26	50.92	56.89	60.55
37	22.01	23.42	26.17	29.44	31.12	44.01	46.51	52.33	58.47	62.23
38	22.60	24.05	26.88	30.24	31.96	45.19	47.77	53.75	60.05	63.91
39	23.19	24.69	27.58	31.03	32.80	46.38	49.03	55.16	61.63	65.59
40	23.79	25.32	28.29	31.83	33.64	47.57	50.29	56.57	63.21	67.28
41	24.38	25.95	29.00	32.62	34.48	48.76	51.54	57.99	64.79	68.96
42	24.98	26.59	29.70	33.42	35.32	49.95	52.80	59.40	66.37	70.64
43	25.57	27.22	30.41	34.21	36.16	51.14	54.06	60.82	67.95	72.32
44	26.17	27.85	31.12	35.01	37.00	52.33	55.31	62.23	69.53	74.00
45	26.76	28.48	31.82	35.80	37.85	53.52	56.57	63.64	71.11	75.69
46	27.36	29.12	32.53	36.60	38.69	54.71	57.83	65.06	72.69	77.37
47	27.95	29.75	33.24	37.40	39.53	55.90	59.08	66.47	74.27	79.05
48	28.55	30.38	33.95	38.19	40.37	57.09	60.34	67.89	75.85	80.73
49	29.14	31.02	34.65	38.99	41.21	58.28	61.60	69.30	77.43	82.41
50	29.74	31.65	35.36	39.78	42.05	59.47	62.86	70.72	79.01	84.09

Exposure Compensation Tables

First Exposure secs	f Stops									
	1.00	1.25	1.33	1.50	1.66	1.75	2.00	2.50	3.00	4.00
1	2.00	2.38	2.52	2.83	3.17	3.37	4.00	5.66	8.00	16.00
2	4.00	4.76	5.03	5.66	6.33	6.73	8.00	11.32	16.00	32.00
3	6.00	7.14	7.55	8.49	9.49	10.10	12.00	16.98	24.00	48.00
4	8.00	9.52	10.06	11.32	12.65	13.46	16.00	22.63	32.00	64.00
5	10.00	11.90	12.58	14.15	15.81	16.82	20.00	28.29	40.00	80.00
6	12.00	14.28	15.09	16.98	18.97	20.19	24.00	33.95	48.00	96.00
7	14.00	16.65	17.60	19.80	22.13	23.55	28.00	39.60	56.00	112.00
8	16.00	19.03	20.12	22.63	25.29	26.91	32.00	45.26	64.00	128.00
9	18.00	21.41	22.63	25.46	28.45	30.28	36.00	50.92	72.00	144.00
10	20.00	23.79	25.15	28.29	31.61	33.64	40.00	56.57	80.00	160.00
11	22.00	26.17	27.66	31.12	34.77	37.00	44.00	62.23	88.00	176.00
12	24.00	28.55	30.17	33.95	37.93	40.37	48.00	67.89	96.00	192.00
13	26.00	30.92	32.69	36.77	41.09	43.73	52.00	73.54	104.00	208.00
14	28.00	33.30	35.20	39.60	44.25	47.10	56.00	79.20	112.00	224.00
15	30.00	35.68	37.72	42.43	47.41	50.46	60.00	84.86	120.00	240.00
16	32.00	38.06	40.23	45.26	50.57	53.82	64.00	90.51	128.00	256.00
17	34.00	40.44	42.74	48.09	53.73	57.19	68.00	96.17	136.00	272.00
18	36.00	42.82	45.26	50.92	56.89	60.55	72.00	101.83	144.00	288.00
19	38.00	45.19	47.77	53.75	60.05	63.91	76.00	107.49	152.00	304.00
20	40.00	47.57	50.29	56.57	63.21	67.28	80.00	113.14	160.00	320.00
21	42.00	49.95	52.80	59.40	66.37	70.64	84.00	118.80	168.00	336.00
22	44.00	52.33	55.31	62.23	69.53	74.00	88.00	124.46	176.00	352.00
23	46.00	54.71	57.83	65.06	72.69	77.37	92.00	130.11	184.00	368.00
24	48.00	57.09	60.34	67.89	75.85	80.73	96.00	135.77	192.00	384.00
25	50.00	59.47	62.86	70.72	79.01	84.09	100.00	141.43	200.00	400.00
26	52.00	61.84	65.37	73.54	82.17	87.46	104.00	147.08	208.00	416.00
27	54.00	64.22	67.88	76.37	85.33	90.82	108.00	152.74	216.00	432.00
28	56.00	66.60	70.40	79.20	88.49	94.19	112.00	158.40	224.00	448.00
29	58.00	68.98	72.91	82.03	91.65	97.55	116.00	164.05	232.00	464.00
30	60.00	71.36	75.43	84.86	94.81	100.91	120.00	169.71	240.00	480.00
31	62.00	73.74	77.94	87.69	97.97	104.28	124.00	175.37	248.00	496.00
32	64.00	76.11	80.45	90.51	101.13	107.64	128.00	181.02	256.00	512.00
33	66.00	78.49	82.97	93.34	104.29	111.00	132.00	186.68	264.00	528.00
34	68.00	80.87	85.48	96.17	107.45	114.37	136.00	192.34	272.00	544.00
35	70.00	83.25	88.00	99.00	110.61	117.73	140.00	197.99	280.00	560.00
36	72.00	85.63	90.51	101.83	113.77	121.09	144.00	203.65	288.00	576.00
37	74.00	88.01	93.02	104.66	116.93	124.46	148.00	209.31	296.00	592.00
38	76.00	90.38	95.54	107.49	120.09	127.82	152.00	214.97	304.00	608.00
39	78.00	92.76	98.05	110.31	123.25	131.18	156.00	220.62	312.00	624.00
40	80.00	95.14	100.57	113.14	126.41	134.55	160.00	226.28	320.00	640.00
41	82.00	97.52	103.08	115.97	129.57	137.91	164.00	231.94	328.00	656.00
42	84.00	99.90	105.59	118.80	132.73	141.28	168.00	237.59	336.00	672.00
43	86.00	102.28	108.11	121.63	135.89	144.64	172.00	243.25	344.00	688.00
44	88.00	104.66	110.62	124.46	139.05	148.00	176.00	248.91	352.00	704.00
45	90.00	107.03	113.14	127.28	142.21	151.37	180.00	254.56	360.00	720.00
46	92.00	109.41	115.65	130.11	145.37	154.73	184.00	260.22	368.00	736.00
47	94.00	111.79	118.16	132.94	148.53	158.09	188.00	265.88	376.00	752.00
48	96.00	114.17	120.68	135.77	151.69	161.46	192.00	271.53	384.00	768.00
49	98.00	116.55	123.19	138.60	154.85	164.82	196.00	277.19	392.00	784.00
50	100.00	118.93	125.71	141.43	158.01	168.18	200.00	282.85	400.00	800.00

Mixing your own chemicals

If you would like to make your own B &W processing solutions, the following notes will be of interest. The developer here is based on the world famous Kodak D 76 formula This developer, like Ilford's ID-11, this developer allows full emulsion speed and delivers excellent shadow detail, normal contrast, and produces fine grain from continuous-tone black & white films.

All of the chemicals listed here are available form most good photographic suppliers. A word of warning here though – you must use **photographic quality chemicals**. Ordinary industrial chemicals are not necessarily of the correct fineness of quality and may adversely affect your films.

The ingredients for D-76 include the following

Water	750 millilitres
Metol or Elon Developing Agent	2 grams
Hydroquinone	5 grams
Sodium Sulfite (anhydrous)	100 grams
Borax	2 grams
Water to make	1 litre

- Heat the water up to 50°C (125°F) and pour 750 mi llilitres into a suitable container.

- Carefully add each of the ingredients in the order that they are listed above and stir thoroughly at each stage to ensure the chemicals are mixed.

- Introduce powder slowly as you stir to ensure it mixes well. When the Borax has been added and stirred add water to make the solution up to 1 litre.

- This is a stock solution that can then be diluted one part water to one part D-76 to give the working developer. When diluted you obtain greater sharpness, but with a slight increase in grain.

The recommended processing temperature for this is 20°C and all times quoted below are in minutes and based on the developer being used at this temperature

Darkroom Data Guide

Development Times

Film	Time
AgfaPan 25	13
AgfaPan 100	13.5
AgfaPan 400	11
Fuji Neopan 400	9.5
Fuji Neopan 1600	9
Ilford Delta 100	11
Ilford Delta 400	10.5
Ilford Delta 400N	14
Ilford Delta 3200	10.5 (neat)
Ilford FP4+	8
Ilford HP5+	13
Ilford Pan F+	81/2
Ilford Plus-X Pan	7
Ilford SFX	17
Kodak Technical Pan	7
Kodak High Speed Infrared	11
Kodak T-Max 100	12
Kodak T-Max 400	12 1/2
Kodak T-Max 3200	14
Kodak Plus X Pan	7
Kodak Tri-X Pan	10
Konica IR750	8.5
Paterson Acupan 200	4
Paterson Acupan 800	11.5

Darkroom Data Guide

Stop Bath

The formula is as follows:

Water 1 litre

Acetic Acid 48 ml (28% solution)

Heat the water up to 32°C (90°F) and carefully add th e acetic acid. Acetic acid is volatile so it must be handled with extreme caution.

Do not inhale and do not add the water to the acetic acid.

This can cause the acetic acid to boil and will spit out in all directions.

General purpose fixer

The ingredients are as follows

Water	600 millilitres
Sodium Thiosulfate (crystaline)	250 grams
Sodium Sulfite (anhydrous)	15 grams
28% Acetic Acid	17millilitres
Boric Acid (crystaline)	7.5 grams
Potassium Alum	15 grams
Cold water to make	1 litre

- Heat the water to 50° C (125° F) then pour 600 mill ilitres into a suitable container.
- Carefully add each of the ingredients in the order that they are listed above and stir thoroughly at each stage to ensure the chemicals are mixed.
- Introduce powder slowly as you stir to ensure it mixes well. When the Potassium Alum has been added and stirred add cold water to make the solution up to 1 litre.

Use the fixer neat (not diluted) at 20°C (68°F). Fi x the film for up to 15 minutes and discard after use. You can check that the film is fixed by holding it up to light. If there are any signs of cloudiness continue to fix until this has cleared.

Wash the film as previously described and use a final rinsing solution of water with a drop of wetting agent added.

Darkroom Data Guide

Faults on Black and White negatives

Fault	Cause	Cure	Prevention
No image formed. Edge numbers and manufacturers name missing.	Film has been put in fixer first instead of developer.	None	Make sure processing is carried out in correct order. Adopt methodical working practice.
Film completely black including edges.	Film completely fogged by light before or during development.	None	Check that all loading and processing stages will not allow film to be fogged. Check that camera is loaded correctly and is light tight.
Film has black frame at beginning but rest of film is clear. Edge markings present. Sprocket holes may be torn.	Camera has not advanced film	None	Check for camera fault.
Film has overlapping double exposed images.	Exposed film has been run through the camera again.	None	Identify exposed films with label or marker pen.
Film is completely clear. Edge markings normal.	Film was unexposed. Edge markings indicate processing was correct.	None	As above.
Bands of uneven density (usually along complete length of film).	Insufficient quantities of developer used.	None	Make sure enough developer is used to completely cover film.
Clear or opal patches .	Film has come into contact with another surface and prevented development. Can be caused by film coils touching.	None	Make sure film is correctly loaded into spirals in tank.

51

Darkroom Data Guide

Faults on Black and White negatives

Fault	Cause	Cure	Prevention
Black bar right across film.	Fogging by light.	None	Check camera back. Cassette may be faulty.
Pale or weak (thin) image. Very Little shadow detail. Edge markings normal.	Film underexposed.	Can be printed but shadow areas may print solid black without any detail.	Check ISO setting on camera.
Negative very dense. Edge markings normal.	Film overexposed.	Can be printed but white areas may be lacking in tone and featureless.	As above.
Negative thin but more shadow detail than when film is underexposed. Low contrast. Edge markings may be weak.	Underdevelopment. 1.Development time too short. 2.Development temperature too low. 3.Insufficient agitation. 4.Developer too weak. 5.Developer exhausted or oxidised.	May be printed but shadow areas will show little detail.	1,2 Check for correct development time, 3,4 Check for correct temperature, agitation and dilution. 5, Use fresh developer.
Image dense and constrasty	Overdevelopment Development time too long. Development temperature too high Excessive agitation. Developer mixed too strong.	Can be printed on soft grade of paper, but grain may be more noticeable.	Check for correct development time, temperature, agitation and dilution.

52

Darkroom Data Guide

Faults on Black and White negatives

Fault	Cause	Cure	Prevention
Film has partial or overall grey fog.	Fogged before development. Film loaded in poorly blacked out darkroom.	If fogging is overall try printing. Bad fog may be treated with chemical reduction.	Check film loading procedure. Check for light tightness of darkroom.
Partial or overall grey fog. Edgelines around sprocket holes.	Film fogged during development.	None.	Check development tank lid is secured and light tight.
Film underdeveloped with possible yellow stain.	Developer exhausted or contaminated.	None.	Do not over use developer. Adopt clean methodical working procedure.
Areas around sprocket holes show uneven density.	Surge Marks. Film has been agitated too severely during development.	None.	Consult manufacturers data for correct agitation procedure.
Film has a milky/ yellow appearance. Overall fogged effect.	Insufficient fixing. 1 Fixing time too short. 2 Fixing temperature too low. 3 Insufficient agitation. 4 Fixer mixed too weak 5 Fixer exhausted 6 Fixer contaminated by developer.	Re-fix film in fresh fixer followed by final wash.	1.2 3.4.Check for correct fixing time, temperature, agitation and dilution. 5. Use fresh fixer. 6. Use stop bath after developing to avoid excessive carry over of developer into fixer.

53

Darkroom Data Guide

Faults on Black and White negatives

Fault	Cause	Cure	Prevention
Edges of film fogged.	Film fogged by light. 1 Film cassette left in strong light before or after exposing. 2 Rollfilm wound too loosely on spool.	None.	1 Always keep cassette in film tub before and after exposing. 2 Wind rollfilm tightly on to spool. Store them away from light.
Film has an overall orange/brown stain.	Probably a colour film has been processed in Black and White chemistry.	Print on Panchromatic paper.	Make sure you always identify films before processing.
Negative shows part of image only.	Probably caused by setting too fast a speed on camera when using flash.	None.	When using flash, make sure you use the correct flash synch speed (or a slower speed).

Darkroom Data Guide

Faults on Black and White negatives

Fault	Cause	Cure	Prevention

Darkroom Data Guide

Faults on Black and White negatives

Fault	Cause	Cure	Prevention

Darkroom Data Guide

Faults on Colour Negatives C41 Process

Fault	Cause	Cure	Prevention
Negatives thin and lacking in contrast. Film edge markings normal.	Film has been underexposed.	None - but may still be printed. Shadow areas will be dull and lifeless.	Check correct ISO setting on camera. Check if exposure compensation has inadvertently been used.
As above but film edge markings are also weak or faint.	Film has been underdeveloped. 1 Development time too short. 2 Development temperature too low. 3 Insufficient agitation. 4 Developer mixed too weak. 5 Developer exhausted. 6 Chemicals out of date.	None - print will be dull and flat. Highlights may have slight yellow cast.	Check for correct development time temperature and agitation. Check for correct dilution of developer. If all else fails, increase development time progressively until correct result achieved.
Negative dense and contrasty. Unexposed areas of film abnormally dark.	A) Overdevelopment. 1 Development temperature too long. 2 Development time too high 3 Excessive agitation. 4 Developer mixed too strong. B) May also be caused by contamination of developer with bleach/fixer.	None - will give print with harsh dark shadow areas and bleached out highlights. Grain will also be more pronounced.	A) Check for correct development time, temperature, and agitation. Check for correct dilution of developer. If all else fails, reduce development time progressively until correct result achieved.
Highlights dense and solid.	Film has been overexposed.	None-will print with featureless and bleached out highlights	B) Try to achieve a clean methodical approach in mixing chemicals and processing. Check for correct camera settings as above.

Darkroom Data Guide

Faults on Colour Negatives C41 Process

Fault	Cause	Cure	Prevention
Overall colour cast and cyan staining.	Developing tank damp with fixer before processing.	None.	Always make sure developing tank is clean and dry before processing.
Negative very dense with brown stains.	Insufficient bleach/fixing. 1 Bleaching/fixing time too short. 2 Bleaching/fixing temperature too low. 3 Insufficient agitation. 4 Bleach/Fixer mixed too weak. 5 Solution exhausted or chemicals out of date.	None.	As in other cases, check processing times, temperatures, agitation techniques etc.
Uneven, irregular development. Stained areas.	Most likely cause is film coils touching during development.	None.	Make sure that film is correctly loaded onto spiral. To prevent film jamming during loading, trim off the leader and chamfer ends of film as described elsewhere.
Negatives have overall green cast.	Film has been exposed to red safelight or red L.E.D's before processing.	None	It is always advisable to load films into tanks in complete darkness. Check darkroom to ensure there are no light leaks.
Negatives have overall cyan cast.	Film has been exposed to brown safelight before processing.	None	Even L.E.D's on darkroom equipment or radios etc can cause this effect. Tape over them or turn them off. If darkroom is suspect then either seal off light, leaks or use a changing bag to load film.
Partial or overall brown cast.	Film has been fogged by white light.	None.	As above but also check that lid of tank is firmly sealed.

58

Faults on Colour Negatives C41 Process

Fault	Cause	Cure	Prevention
Film is contrasty and has an overall purple cast.	Colour slide film has been processed by mistake.	None - but try printing a few for a surreal effect. Accidents like this can sometimes give rise to an unexpected and pleasing result	Always check that you are processing the right film. The film canister always states the type of process required.

Darkroom Data Guide

Faults on Colour Negatives C41 Process

Fault	Cause	Cure	Prevention

Darkroom Data Guide

Faults on Processing Colour Transparencies E6 Process

Fault	Cause	Cure	Prevention
Image thin, lacking in contrast, possible blue cast. Border edges weak and thin.	Overdeveloped in First developer 1 Developing time too long. 2 Developing temperature too high. 3 Developer mixed too strong. 4 Too much agitation. 5 Stop bath missed out or exhausted. 6 First wash too long.	None	Check for correct dilution, temperature and time. Use correct agitation procedure. If all else fails, progressively reduce first development time.
Colours weak, blue overall cast, border edges weak and thin.	Underdeveloped in colour developer. ' 1 Developing time too short. 2 Developing temperature too low. 3 Insufficient agitation. 4 Developer exhausted. 5 Developer mixed too weak. 6 Chemicals out of date.	None	Check for correct dilution, temperature and time. Use correct agitation procedure.
Film appears to be milky after drying.	Insufficient fixing. 1 Fixing time too short. 2 Fixing temperature too low 3 Fixer mixed too weak. 4 Fixer exhausted.	Film should be re-fixed and washed.	Check for correct dilution, temperature and time. Use correct agitation procedure.
Image thin and weak with Cyan cast.	Colour developer contaminated with First developer	None	Be careful to avoid cross contamination between chemicals. Thoroughly wash measures/ beaker between mixing different chemicals. If possible, use a separate measure/ beaker for each chemical and mark them for easy identification.

61

Darkroom Data Guide

Faults on Processing Colour Transparencies E6 Process

Fault	Cause	Cure	Prevention
Image dense and dark, possible magenta cast.	Underdeveloped in first developer. 1 Developing time too short. 2 Developing time too low. 3 Insufficient agitation. 4 Developer exhausted. 5 Developer mixed too weak. 6 Chemicals out of date.	None	Check for correct dilution, temperature and time. Use correct agitation procedure. If all else fails, progressively increase first development time.
Overall red or yellow cast.	Overdeveloped in colour developer. 1 Development time too long. 2 Development temperature too high. 3 Developer mixed too strong. 4 Too much agitation. 5 Stop bath missed out or exhausted.	None	Check for correct dilution, temperature and time. Use correct agitation procedure. If all else fails, progressively reduce colour development time.
Film has overall red cast or partial red cast with other areas normal.	Film loaded while exposed to red light. e.g. black and white darkroom safe light on, or L.E.D's on radios or darkroom equipment etc, have affected film.	None	Ensure complete darkness while loading. Switch off all equipment likely to cause problems, or apply tape to cover L.E.D's.
Heavy overall blue cast, borders weak and thin.	First developer contaminated with stop bath.	None	Avoid cross contamination as above.
Magenta spots or clusters on film.	Air bubbles have clung to film surface during first development.	None	Immediately after pouring first developer into tank, tap tank on bench to dislodge air bubbles.

62

Darkroom Data Guide

Faults on Processing Colour Transparencies E6 Process

Fault	Cause	Cure	Prevention
Red spots or areas on film.	Stop bath or fixer has been splashed onto film after it has been dried.	Re-wash and dry film. Re-wash film in solution of salt water. (1 tablespoon of salt to 1 pint of water) Then re-wash and dry as normal.	Avoid splashing chemicals.
Brown stains on film.	Insufficient bleaching. 1 Bleaching time too short. 2 Bleaching temperature too low. 3 Insufficient agitation. 4 Bleach exhausted. 5 Bleach mixed too weak. 6 Chemicals out of date.	Re-bleach, fix and wash.	Check for correct dilution, temperature and time. Use correct agitation procedure.
Crazy paving effect over film emulsion surface.	Caused by too sudden a temperature change. Sometimes caused by washing film in very cold tap water immediately after processing.	None	If possible use water at same temperature used in processing. If not possible, wash film in progressively colder water, decreasing the water temperature in steps of 5 degrees (Celsius) maximum per wash.
Uneven, irregular development with possibly stained areas.	Film coils touching during development	None.	Check that film is being correctly loaded onto film spiral. Cut off film leader to leave square edge and chamfer corners to avoid film jamming during loading.

63

Darkroom Data Guide

Faults on Processing Colour Transparencies E6 Process

Fault	Cause	Cure	Prevention

Darkroom Data Guide

Faults on Processing Colour Transparencies E6 Process

Fault	Cause	Cure	Prevention

Darkroom Data Guide

Faults on Black and White Prints

Fault	Cause	Cure	Prevention
Unsharp overall.	1 Enlarger not focused properly. 2 Focus has slipped. 3 Enlarger head has slipped. 4 Negative has 'popped'. 5 Vibration.	None	1 Focus more carefully. Use focus finder. Check own eyesight. 2 Check and tighten focusing mechanism. 3 Tighten enlarger head. 4 Refocus after enlarger has warmed up. 5 Use firmer support for enlarger. Don't move around during exposure.
Not sharp at top or bottom, or on one side of print.	1 Negative incorrectly positioned in carrier. 2 Negative carrier not parallel to baseboard. 3 Lens board not parallel to baseboard. 4 Enlarger head not parallel to baseboard.	None	1 Check negative is supported properly. 2 Check negative carrier is correctly inserted and positioned. 3 Check for correct lens board location. Tighten lens board retaining screws. 4 Adjust head to zero position, tighten lockscrew.
Unsharp at centre, while edges are sharp or vice versa.	1 Negative has 'popped'. 2 Lens aperture too large giving insufficient depth of field to cover curvature of negative. 3 Negative incorrectly held in carrier.	None	1 Refocus after enlarger has warmed up. 2 Stop down lens 2 or 3 stops more. 3 Check negative is properly held in carrier.
Fuzzy, double or multiple image in some areas. Other areas sharp.	1 Focus has moved during exposure. 2 Negative has 'popped'.	None	1 Refocus, check and tighten head and focus controls. 2 Refocus after enlarger head has warmed up.

66

Darkroom Data Guide

Faults on Black and White Prints

Fault	Cause	Cure	Prevention
Double or multiple image.	1 Enlarger head has slipped. 2 Focus has slipped. 3 Negative accidentally moved during exposure 4 Negative has 'popped'. 5 Printing paper has been moved during exposure.	None	1 Tighten enlarger head lock. 2 Tighten focussing mechanism. 3 Don't touch negative during exposure. 4 Refocus after enlarger has warmed up. 5 Use proper masking frame. Don't touch paper during exposure.
Print too light.	1 Under-exposure. 2 Under development.	None	1 More exposure required: a) increase time or b) increase lens aperture Use proper test strip method to obtain correct exposure. 2 Check for correct development t ime/ temperature. Developer may be exhausted or contaminated.
Print too dark.	1 Over-exposure. 1 Negative density range too great 1 Negative density range too great	It may be possible to lighten the print by using a chemical reducer	Less exposure required: a) decrease time or b) reduce lens aperture Use proper test strip method to obtain correct exposure.
Print, correct but with some areas tco light.		None	Reprint and 'burn in' light areas.
Print correct but with some areas tco dark.		Use chemical reducer on print locally in dark areas	Reprint and 'shade' or 'dodge' dark areas.

Darkroom Data Guide

Faults on Black and White Prints

Fault	Cause	Cure	Prevention
Print too light towards corners. Overall uneven density.	1 Lamp to condenser distance wrong. 2 Wrong condenser fitted. 3 Wrong light box being used on diffuser enlarger. 4 Wrong focal length lens being used.	None	1 Adjust to give even illumination. 2 Use correct condensers. 3 Use correct light box for format being used. 4 Use correct focal length lens for format: 35mm f = 50mm 6 x 6 f = 80mm 6 x 7 f = 90mm
Varying density especially in shadow areas.	1 Developer exhausted, contaminated or too dilute. 2 Uneven development.	None	1 Mix up fresh developer, check using correct strength. 2 Use sufficient developer. Immerse whole of print quickly. Agitate throughout development period.
Density correct but-print appears grey and lifeless. No pure whites or deep blacks. Flat or soft print.	1 Wrong grade of paper being used. 2 Wrong filters being used with variable contrast papers. 3 Negative under-exposed, or under developed. 4 Exhausted or contaminated print developer. 5 'Snatching' print out of developer too early.	None	1 Use harder grade of paper. 2 Check that correct filters and exposure time have been used. 3 Use harder grade of paper Check manufacturers film exposure and processing instructions. 4 Use new developer. 5 Process print for full development time.
	6 Paper fogged.		6 Check for light leaks in darkroom. Check safety of safelight.

Darkroom Data Guide

Faults on Black and White Prints

Fault	Cause	Cure	Prevention
Density correct but print appears contrasty. Harsh blacks and whites with no mid tones.	1 Wrong grace of paper being used. 2 Wrong filters being used with variable contrast papers. 3 Negative contrast too great due to over development.	None	1 Use softer grade of paper. 2 Check that correct filters and exposure times have been used. 3 Use softer grade of paper. Check manufacturers film and processing instructions.
Overall density and contrast correct but some areas too flat (grey or soft).	Subject lighting range inconsistent E.g. flat lighting in shadow areas while highlights are brightly lit.	None	Reprint with variable contrast paper. Expose print in separate stages, using a higher (harder) grade of filter for flat areas and the same filter to expose the correct density/contrast areas.
Overall density and contrast correct but some areas too hard (contrasty).	1 Subject lighting range inconsistent E.g dense/contrasty shadow areas.	None	Reprint with variable contrast paper. Expose print in separate stages, using a lower (softer) grade of filter for hard areas and the same filter to expose the correct density/contrast areas.
White spots or squiggles sharply defined on print.	Hair, grit or fibre on the negative or printing paper.	If there are many blemishes; reprint Otherwise retouch with spotting fluid	1 Use filtered water for mixing chemicals and washing. 2 Hang film to dry in dust free area Cut and store film after drying as quickly as possible. 3 Blow negative with compressed air. 4 Breathe on shiny side of negative and gently wipe clean with fibre free tissue.
Soft edged round areas of lighter tone on print.	Dirt, or particles on condensers in condenser enlarger.	Retouch or reprint	Inspect and clean condensers before printing session.

Darkroom Data Guide

Faults on Black and White Prints

Fault	Cause	Cure	Prevention
Light parallel lines ending with 'pear drop'.	1 Drying marks - usually on base (shiny) side of film.	Retouch or reprint if excessive	1 Wash and process film using filtered water. 2 Use correct amount of wetting agent in final wash. 3 Use pre-dampened squeegee to remove excess water from film before drying. 4 For stubborn marks, breathe on shiny side of films and gently wipe clean with a fibre free tissue.
Round dark areas surrounded by a light line.	Drying marks on emulsion side of film.	Retouch or reprint if excessive	1 Wash and process film using filtered water. 2 Use correct amount of wetting agent in final wash. 3 Use pre-dampened squeegee to remove excess water from film before drying. 4 NOTE: blemishes cannot easily be removed from emulsion side of film without damaging film emulsion.
1) Black spots or squiggles. 2) Black parallel lines.	1 Dust in camera. 2 Scratches on film from camera or by over use of reloadable cassettes. 3 Scratches on film caused by squeegee.	Retouch or reprint if excessive	1 Clean camera interior with blower brush/compressed air or best of all with a mini vacuum cleaner (Photographic). 2 Check film tracks and pressure plate in camera for rough edges and burrs. 3 Pre-moisten squeegee and run fingers down rubber wiper blades to check for grit.

Darkroom Data Guide

Faults on Black and White Prints

Fault	Cause	Cure	Prevention
Fine black lines with a random pattern.	Stress marks caused by emulsion surface of print being scratched.	Retouch if possible otherwise reprint	Use rubber lipped print tongs.
Bands of concentric light/dark lines usually curved oval or roughly circular.	Newtons rings, usually caused by glass negative carriers.	Difficult to retouch Opt for reprinting	1 Use anti Newton glass in negative carrier. 2 Try cleaning glass carrier thoroughly. Make sure film is pressed hard against glass.
Large unevenly developed areas or mottled effect.	Emulsion surface of print has not been fully under developer.	None	Use sufficient developer Immerse print quickly, face down. Agitate for full development period.

71

Darkroom Data Guide

Faults on Black and White Prints

Fault	Cause	Cure	Prevention

Darkroom Data Guide

Faults on Black and White Prints

Fault	Cause	Cure	Prevention

Darkroom Data Guide

Faults on Colour Prints from Colour Negatives

Fault	Cause	Cure	Prevention
Overall or partial slight pink cast.	Condensation or moisture on paper	None	Allow very cold paper time to warm up before processing.
Yellow stains.	1 Bleach/fix exhausted. 2 Insufficient washing. 3 Drying temperature too high.	1 Try re-bleach/ fix and wash. 2 Re-wash 3 None	1 Check dilution of bleach/fixer. Use fresh chemicals. 2 Check for correct washing time and temperature. 3 Avoid using excessive drying temperatures.
Intense overall Magenta cast or fog.	Developer contaminated with bleach/fixer.	None	1 Avoid cross contamination of chemicals. 2 Use separate measuring cylinders for chemicals.
Left to right reversal of image with pale cyan cast.	Paper exposed emulsion side down.	None.	Practice finding emulsion surface in the dark. If in doubt, put paper between your lips. The emulsion side will stick to one lip.
Cyan stain.	Developer contaminated with bleach/fixer.	None.	Avoid cross contamination of chemicals as above.
Magenta or red spots.	1 Some bleach/fixer splattered onto print at end of processing. 2 Rust or iron particles in water.	1 Try re-washing 2 None	1 Adopt methodical clean working routine. 2 Use filtered water.
Intense overall red/brown cast.	Printing filters omitted, paper exposed to white light.	None	1 Check that printing filters are in place. 2 Check that white light lever is in correct position.

Darkroom Data Guide

Faults on Colour Prints from Colour Negatives

Fault	Cause	Cure	Prevention
Cyan or blue spots.	Bleach or fixer splattered into print developer.	None	Adopt methodical clean working routine.
Magenta or red stain.	Insufficient washing.	Try re-washing.	Always wash for recommended times. 2 Check for correct flow rate in processors.
Multiple spots of several different colours.	Paper contaminated by "fallout" of chemical powder.	None	Mix powders or liquids in a separate area.
Print flat overall with areas of uneven development.	Paper placed in drum, with emulsion side touching drum wall.	None.	Check for correct loading. Identify emulsion surface as above.
Colours distorted. Contrast low, image density weak.	1 Development time too short. 2 Development temperature too low. 3 Developer mixed too weak. 4 Insufficient agitation. 5 Chemicals exhausted or out of date.	None.	Check for correct development time, temperature and agitation. Check for correct dilution. If all else fails, progressively increase development time.
Colours distorted, print too dark with excessive contrast.	1 Development time too long. 2 Developing temperature too high. 3 Developer mixed too strong. 4 Excessive agitation.	None.	Check for correct development time, temperature and agitation. Check for correct dilution. If all else fails, progressively increase development time.
Emulsion surface blistered.	Drying temperature too high.	None	Check print drier temperature, adjust to recommended level.

Darkroom Data Guide

Faults on Colour Prints from Colour Negatives

Fault	Cause	Cure	Prevention
White spots or areas of local low density. (lighter patches).	1 Water/bleach/fixer splashed onto paper before developing. 2 Moisture condensation droplets on surface of paper. 3 Air bubbles on surface of paper, 4 Paper handled with wet or chemical contaminated fingers.	None	1,4 Adopt clean working procedure. 2 Allow cold paper time to warm up before using. 3 Check correct procedure being used.
Bright red areas or scratch like marks chips.	Top layer of paper emulsion has been removed.	None.	1 Check that you are not accidentally scratching the paper surface. 2 Possible fault in paper.
Overall red or magenta mottled effect and possibly streaks as well.	Too much developer being carried over into bleach/fixer plus insufficient agitation.	None.	Try to drain off as much developer as possible before bleaching/fixing. Consult: Manufacturer's instructions on tank, drum etc.
Yellows muddy or dull.	1 Bleach/fixing time too short. 2 Bleach/fixer mixed too weak. 3 Bleach/fixer exhausted.	Try re-bleach/ fixing or reprint	1 Check for correct time, temperature and agitation. 2 Use correct dilution. 3 Use fresh chemicals.
Cyan or "blue streaks or lines.	1 Fog from safelight. 2 Kinks in paper. 3 Emulsion surface abraded or damaged.	None.	1 Run test on safelight. 2 Handle paper more carefully. 3 Avoid accidentally scuffing or scratching emulsion. Possible fault in paper.
Strong cyan or magenta cast. Print generally dark.	Even slight contamination of the developer with bleach/fixer can cause this.	None.	Adopt clean methodical working method.

Darkroom Data Guide

Faults on Colour Prints from Colour Negatives

Fault	Cause	Cure	Prevention
Print normal with lighter areas giving mottled effect.	Moisture condensation on paper. Water droplets or splashes on paper.	None.	Adopt clean methodical working method.
General high stain levels.	1. Print overdeveloped. 2. Developer exhausted. 3. Developer oxidized. 4. Developer contaminated with bleach/fixer. 5. Insufficient washing.	None.	1 Check for correct development time, temperature, dilution and agitation. 2,3,4 Use fresh chemicals. 5 Wash prints for recommended time.
Unsharp overall			
Not sharp at top or bottom, or on one side of print.			
Unsharp at centre, while edges are sharp, or vice versa.	See Black & White Fault Finding Chart for information on all these faults		
Fuzzy, double or multiple images in some areas, other areas sharp.			
Double or multiple images.			
Print too light.			
Print too dark.			

Darkroom Data Guide

Faults on Colour Prints from Colour Negatives

Fault	Cause	Cure	Prevention

Darkroom Data Guide

Faults on Colour Prints from Colour Negatives

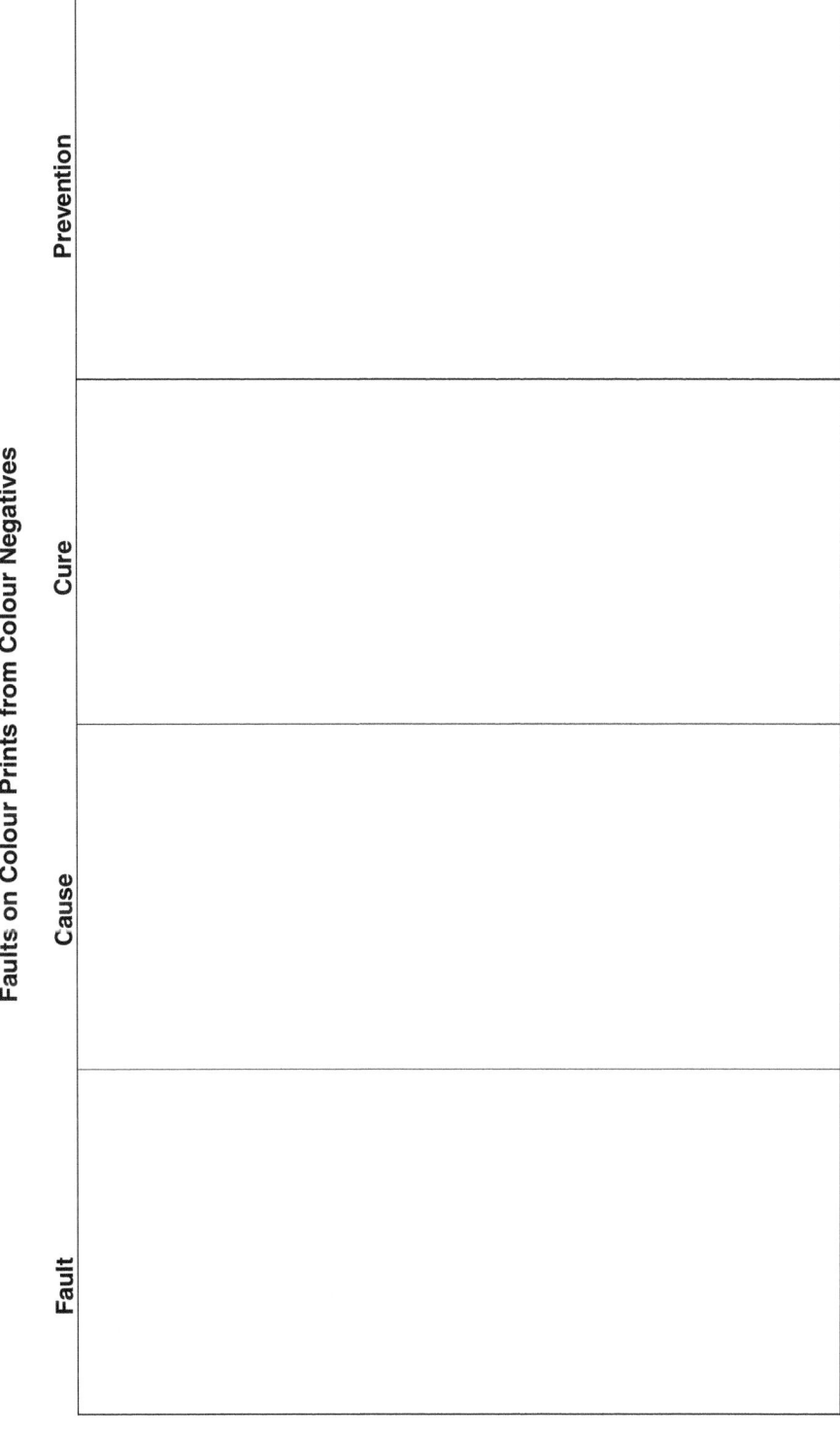

Fault	Cause	Cure	Prevention

Darkroom Data Guide

Faults on Colour Prints from Ilfochrome Classic (Cibachrome)

Fault	Cause	Cure	Prevention
Light marks on print sometimes white.	Paper fogged by stray light.	None	Check darkroom for light tightness. Check that paper is protected from light after opening.
Dark print with heavy orange/red cast.	Paper has been exposed emulsion side down in easel.	None	Make sure you identify the emulsion side of the paper correctly. The brown emulsion side should be facing upwards on the easel. *The base is pure white. If in doubt place paper between your lips. The emulsion side will stick to one of your lips.*
Overall red cast or red areas.	1. Paper has been exposed to red light, e.g. Black and White red/orange safelight left on. 2. Light from red L.E.D's has fogged paper.	None	1. It is safer to work in complete darkness, even if you use correct safelight. 2 Switch off all equipment with L.E.D's e.g. radios etc, or tape over L.E.D's with black tape.
Orange cast over entire print. Blacks tend to be blue.	Developer has been contaminated by fixer.	None.	Ensure clean methodical working practice.
Print dark and flat (dull).	Underdevelopment. 1 Development time too short. 2 Development temperature too low. 3 Insufficient agitation. 4. Chemicals mixed too weak. 5 Developer exhausted. 6 Chemicals out of date.	None.	1,2,3 Check for correct time, temperature and agitation. 4 Check for correct dilution. 5,6 Use fresh chemicals.

Darkroom Data Guide

Faults on Colour Prints from Ilfochrome Classic (Cibachrome)

Fault	Cause	Cure	Prevention
Print *too* light overall but otherwise correct.	Overexposure. Print has been exposed for too long.	None.	Decrease exposure to give clearer print. Use test strip method to determine correct exposure.
Print too dark overall but otherwise correct.	Underexposure. Print has not received sufficient exposure.	None.	Increase exposure to give lighter print. Use test strip method to determine correct exposure.
Print light with low density.	Overdevelopment. 1 Development time too long. 2 Development temperature too high. 3 Excessive agitation. 4 Chemicals mixed too strong.	None.	1,2,3 Check for correct time, temperature and agitation. 4 Check for correct dilution.
Print has grey areas and poor bleaching. Many show uneven development.	Insufficient processing solution.	None.	Usually occurs when using a drum for processing. Make sure sufficient solution quantities are used. Make sure drum is horizontal.
Uneven, patchy development.	Emulsion surface touching wall of drum.	None.	Check for correct drum loading procedure. Make sure emulsion surface of paper faces inwards in drum.
Print, dark, fogged and dull.	Fixing carried out before bleaching.	None.	Adopt methodical working procedure.

81

Darkroom Data Guide

Faults on Colour Prints from Ilfochrome Classic (Cibachrome)

Fault	Cause	Cure	Prevention
Print has overall dark, dull and milky appearance.	1 Insufficient bleaching time. 2 Bleach solution too weak.	None.	1 Check for correct processing times, temperatures and agitation. 2 Check for correct dilution.
Print black overall, with barely visible image.	Bleaching step has been omitted.	None.	Adopt methodical working procedure.
Print flat and dull with yellow cast.	Fixing step has been omitted.	Repeat fixing step followed by final wash.	Adopt methodical working procedure.
Print has light blue cast. Maximum density areas weak.	Developer too concentrated.	None.	Check for correct dilution.
Blacks have a brown cast, unexposed borders brown/black or local brown stains	1 Bleaching time insufficient. 2 Bleach solution mixed too weak. 3 Bleach exhausted.	Re-bleach for correct time or use fresh bleach, followed by re-fixing and washing.	1,2 Make sure you are using correct bleaching time and dilution. 3 Use fresh bleach.

Darkroom Data Guide

Faults on Colour Prints from Ilfochrome Classic (Cibachrome)

Fault	Cause	Cure	Prevention

Darkroom Data Guide

Faults on Colour Prints from Ilfochrome Classic (Cibachrome)

Fault	Cause	Cure	Prevention

ILFORD FILM PROCESSING CHART

20°C/68°F		PAN F PLUS		FP4 PLUS			HP5 PLUS						DELTA 100 PRO			DELTA 400 PROFESSIONAL								DELTA 3200 PROFESSIONAL						SFX 200		
	EI	25	50	50	125	200	250	320	400	800	1600	3200	50	100	200	200	250	320	400	500	800	1600	3200	400	800	1600	3200	6400	12500	200	400	800
ILFOTEC DD-X	1+4	7	8	8	10	12			9	10	13	20	9½	12	14	6			8	9½	10½	13½	18	6	7	8	9½	12½	17	10	14	
ID-11	stock	4½	6½	6½	8½	10			7½	10½	14		7	8½	10½	7			9½		11½	14½	19	7	8	9½	10½	13	17	10	14	18
	1+1	6	8½	8	11	15			13	16½			10	11	13	10			14		17½									17		
	1+3	12½	15	17	20				20				15	20		18																
ILFOTEC HC	1+15				4	5				5	7½	11						4			5½	7½	13			5	8	13		5	7	10½
	1+31		4	6	8	9			6½	9½	14		5	6	8	5			7½		10	13½		6	7½	9	14½			9	13	19
ILFOTEC LC29	1+9				4	5				5	7½	11						4			5½	7½	13			5	8	13		5	7	10½
	1+19		4	6	8	9			6½	9½	14		5	6	8	5			7½		10	13½		6	7½	9	14½			9	13	19
	1+29		5½	8	12				9				5½	7½	10	8½			11½		17									11		
ILFOSOL S	1+9		4	4½	6½	7½			7	8½	14		4½	6		6½			9		14			6½	8	10½	13			9½	11½	19
	1+14		6	7½	9½				9½	14			6½	10		10			13											13	19	
MICROPHEN	stock	–	4½		8	9			6½	8	11	16		6½	8	5			6½	7½	8½	10½	14	6	7	8	9	12	16½	8½	10½	14½
	1+1	–	6		10	14			12	15				10	14	8½			11½	13½	15½	19								15½	19	
	1+3	–	11		14	18			23					14	20	16																
PERCEPTOL	stock	9	14	9	12		13						12	15		10	12							11	13	15	18			14½		
	1+1	10½	15	13	15			18					13	17		12½		15½												20		
	1+3	15	17	17	21			25					16	22		18½																
ACUFINE	stock				4	6			4½	6½	9½				5½	7			9	11	13	16										
RODINAL	1+25		6		9	13			6	8			7	9		6½			9					5½	7	9	11	20				
	1+50		11		15	20			11				10	14		11			20													
D-76	stock	4½	6½	6	8	9			7½	9½	12½		7	9	11	7			9½		11½	14½	19	7	8	9½	10½	13	17	10	12½	16½
	1+1	6	8½	9	11	15			11	13			9½	12	14	10			14		17½									14½		
	1+3	12½	15	14	16	20			22				14	22		18																
HC 110 A	1+15				4½	6					5½	9½						4			5½	7½	13			5	8	13		5		
HC 110 B	1+31		4	6	9	12			5	7½	11		5	6	8				7½		10	13½		6	7½	9	14½			9		
MICRODOL-X	stock	12	15	10	15								12	15		11		13½						10	11½	13	18					
	1+3	15	18	17	23								16	22																		
T-MAX	1+4		4		8	9			6½	8	9½	11½	6	7	8	5			6½	7	8½	10½	13½	5½	6½	7½	8½	11	14	8½	10½	12½
XTOL	stock	5½	6¾		8½	10			8	11	14	19	6½	7½	9½	6			7½	8½	10	13	17	5	6	6½	7½	10	12½	7	11	
	1+1								12	17						9			11½	13	15½	20										

DEVELOPMENT TIMES
Follow the recommended times in the chart for the film/developer combination of your choice.

CAUTION:
These times are intended as a **guide only.** Times shorter than 5 minutes may lead to uneven development.

AGITATION
For manual processing in spiral tanks and deep tanks, the development times are based on intermittent agitation. With spiral tanks, invert the tank four times during the first 10 seconds, then invert the tank four times again during the first 10 seconds for each further minute. Where continuous agitation is used for manual processing (as in a dish/tray or with some types of developing tank), reduce these times by up to 15%. For use in rotary processors without a pre-rinse, reduce the spiral tank development times by up to 15%. A pre-rinse is not recommended as it can lead to uneven processing.

FIXATION
After development, rinse the film in water or ILFORD ILFOSTOP or ILFOSTOP PRO stop bath (1+19) for 10 seconds at 20°C/68°F, and fix in ILFORD HYPAM or ILFORD RAPID FIXER (1+4) for 2–5 minutes at 20°C/68°F.

WASHING
Where a non-hardening fixer, such as HYPAM or ILFORD RAPID FIXER, has been used, wash the film in running water for 5–10 minutes at a temperature within 5°C/9°F of the processing temperature.

Some products in this chart may not be available in your country.

01074.GB.www August 2004

Ilfotec DD-X, IlfotecLC29 and Ilfosol S Film Developers

Liquid concentrate developers for low volume black and white film processing in spiral tanks, dishes/trays and rotary processors without replenishment

ILFORD ILFOTEC DD-X, ILFOTEC LC29 and ILFOSOL S are a range of liquid concentrate film developers formulated to exploit the full potential of conventional black and white film emulsions in all formats. They enable professionals and amateurs to develop small quantities of ILFORD and other films with ease and convenience. Their versatility allows for the optimization of individual film speed, quality and economy while performing consistently throughout their long working lives.

Ilford ilfotec DD-X

ILFORD ILFOTEC DD-X is an excellent fine grain developer which gives full film speed. It produces negatives which are easy to print. Correctly exposed negatives developed in ILFOTEC DD-X have a full range of tones, with depth in the shadows, a smooth transition through the mid-tones and bright detailed highlights.

ILFOTEC DD-X is designed to complement the features of all ILFORD films, especially the range of ILFORD DELTA PROFESSIONAL films. In particular it is recommended for use with DELTA 3200 PROFESSIONAL film rates at EI 3200/36. It also gives excellent results when used with quality black and white films from other manufacturers.

ILFOTEC DD-X ensures a good balance of fine grain, sharpness and tonal rendition producing negatives which allow a high degree of enlargement. In addition it is highly recommended when fast films need to be push processed such as HP5 Plus, DELTA 400 PROFESSIONAL, DELTA 3200 PROFESSIONAL and SFX200.

ILFOTEC DD-X is supplied as a liquid concentrate diluted 1+4 for one-shot use when the highest image quality is required. However, for greater economy it can be reused but image quality will be reduced slightly.

Ilford ilfotec LC29

ILFORD ILFOTEC LC29 is a high dilution liquid concentrate black and white film developer that is flexible and economic to use. It is based on the technology used in ILFORD ILFOTEC HC developer but is formulated to be an easy to pour liquid for small volume film processing.

Ilford Powder Developers

ILFORD PERCEPTOL, ID-11 and MICROPHEN powder developers have been formulated to exploit the full potential of conventional black and white film emulsions in all formats. These developers enable ILFORD and other films to be developed to optimize their individual speed and quality and show consistency in performance throughout their long working lives.

PERCEPTOL it an extra fine grain film developer which gives excellent image quality. It is designed for use when very fine grain negatives are required and a decrease in film speed is not important. It has been specially formulated to get optimum results from high resolution lenses. It exploits the superb grain structure of ILFORD medium and slow speed films, 10O DELTA PROFESSIONAL, FP4 Plus and PAN F Plus, and produces significantly finer grain in ILFORD fast films, DELTA 400 PROFESSIONAL, HP5 Plus and DELTA 3200 PROFESSIONAL, compared with a standard fine grain developer.

PERCEPTOL produces excellent results with any lens/film combination and is therefore ideal when texture and definition are critical. Negatives developed in PERCEPTOL are capable of producing sharper and better quality enlargements than those produced using a standard fine grain developer.

ILFORD ID-11 is a fine grain film developer for all general film processing requirements where fine grain negatives are required without loss of emulsion speed. ID-11 developer is recognized internationally as a standard in many fields of scientific and technical photography.

ID-11 produces excellent results with all films and is ideal where a wide range of films and film speeds have been used. ID-11 ensures the best balance of fine grain, sharpness and tonal rendition producing negatives which allow a high degree of enlargement.

ILFORD MICROPHEN is a fine grain film developer which gives an effective increase in film speed. A speed increase of up to half a stop can be achieved with most films but with faster films such as HP5 Plus, Delta 400 Professional and Delta 3200 Professional it is greater. Many developers that give an increase in film speed usually produce a corresponding increase in grain size. MICROPHEN, however, is formulated to overcome this disadvantage as the low alkalinity of the developer reduces grain size and grain clumping. Therefore MICROPHEN is said to have a high speed/grain ratio, i.e. it gives a speed increase while retaining much of the grain characteristics associated with fine grain developers.

MICROPHEN is particularly useful when using extended development times to push process fast films such as HP5 Plus, Delta 400 Professional, Delta 3200 Professional and SFX200.

Ilford Powder Developers for Ilford Films

POWDER DEVELOPERS

ILFORD films

Temperature 20°C/68°F
Time in minutes

Developer	Meter setting	PERCEPTOL			ID-11			MICROPHEN		
Dilution		stock	1+1	1+3	stock	1+1	1+3	stock	1+1	1+3
DELTA 100 PROFESSIONAL	EI 50/18	12	13	16	7	10	15	–	–	–
	EI 100/21	15	17	22	8.30	11	20	6.30	10	14
	EI 200/24	–	–	–	10.30	13	–	8	14	20
DELTA 400 PROFESSIONAL	EI 200/24	10	12.30	18.30	7	10	18	5	8.30	16
	EI 250/25	12	–	–	–	–	–	–	–	–
	EI 320/26	–	15.30	–	–	–	–	–	–	–
	EI 400/27	–	–	–	9.30	14	–	6.30	11.30	–
	EI 500/28	–	–	–	–	–	–	7.30	13.30	–
	EI 800/30	–	–	–	11.30	17.30	–	8.30	15.30	–
	EI 1600/33	–	–	–	14.30	–	–	10.30	19	–
	EI 3200/36	–	–	–	19	–	–	14		
DELTA 3200 PROFESSIONAL	EI 400/27	11	–	–	7	–	–	6	–	–
	EI 800/30	13	–	–	8	–	–	7	–	–
	EI 1600/33	15	–	–	9.30	–	–	8	–	–
	EI 3200/36	18	–	–	10.30	–	–	9	–	–
	EI 6400 /39	–	–	–	13	–	–	12	–	–
	EI 12500/42	–	–	–	17	–	–	16.30	–	–
	EI 25000/45	–	–	–	–	–	–	17.30	–	–
PANF Plus	EI 25/15	9	10.30	15	4.30	6	12.30	–	–	–
	EI 50/18	14	15	17	6.30	8.30	15	4.30	6	11
	EI 64/19	–	–	–	–	–	–	6	9	14.30
FP4 Plus	EI 50/18	9	13	17	6.30	8	17	–	–	–
	EI 125/22	12	15	21	8.30	11	20	8	10	14
	EI 200 /24	–	–	–	10	15	–	9	14	18
HP5 Plus	EI 250/25	13	–	–	–	–	–	–	–	–
	EI 320/26	–	18	25	–	–	–	–	–	–
	EI 400/27	–	–	–	7.30	13	20	6.30	12	23
	EI 800/30	–	–	–	10.30	16.30	–	8	15	–
	EI 1600/33	–	–	–	14	–	–	11	–	–
	EI 3200/36	–	–	–	–	–	–	16	–	–
SFX 200	EI 200/24	14.30	20	–	10	17	–	8.30	15.30	–
	EI 400/27	–	–	–	14	–	–	10.30	19	–
	EI 800/30	–	–	–	18	–	–	14.30	–	–
ORTHO PLUS Pictorial Contrast	EI 80/20 Daylight									
	Normal	–	–	–	8	10.30	16	9	11.30	13.30
	High	–	–	–	10	13	20	12	14.30	17
	EI 40/17 Tungsten									
	Normal	–	–	–	8	10.3	16	9	11.3	13.3
	High	–	–	–	10	13	20	12	14.3	17

Ilford Powder Developers for non Ilford Films

POWDER DEVELOPERS

Non-ILFORD films

Temperature 20°C/68°F
Time in minutes

Developer	Meter setting	PERCEPTOL stock	1+1	1+3	ID-11 stock	1+1	1+3	MICROPHEN stock	1+1	1+3
Kodak Tmax 100	EI 100/21	12	13	19	8	11	16	8	11	16
	EI 200/24	–	–	–	–	–	–	–	–	–
Kodak Tmax 400	EI 400/27	11	12	17	7	10	15	7	10	15
	EI 800/30	–	–	–	9.30	–	–	–	–	–
	EI 1600/33	–	–	–	12	–	–	–	–	–
	EI 3200/36	–	–	–	15	–	–	–	–	–
	EI 6400/39	–	–	–	18	–	–	–	–	–
Kodak Tmax 3200	EI 400/27	–	–	–	–	–	–	–	–	–
	EI 800/30	–	–	–	–	–	–	–	–	–
	EI 1600/33	–	–	–	11	–	–	9	–	–
	EI 3200/36	–	–	–	14	–	–	12	–	–
	EI 6400/39	–	–	–	–	–	–	14	–	–
Kodak Plus X	EI 64/19	8	8.30	12	–	–	–	–	–	–
	EI 125/22	–	–	–	7	8	13	–	–	–
	EI 200/24	–	–	–	–	–	–	6	8.30	13.30
Kodak Tri X	EI 200/24	10	12	15	–	–	–	–	–	–
	EI 400/27	–	–	–	7.30	11	19	–	–	–
	EI 500/28	–	–	–	–	–	–	6	11	22
	EI 800/30	–	–	–	–	–	–	–	–	–
	EI 1600/33	–	–	–	12	–	–	–	–	–
Agfa APX 100	EI 50/18	9	–	–	–	–	–	–	–	–
	EI 100/21	–	–	–	9	13.30	–	–	–	–
	EI 200/24	–	–	–	–	–	–	9	–	–
Agfa APX 400	EI 320/26	14	17	24	–	–	–	–	–	–
	EI 400/27	–	–	–	10	14.30	25	10.30	19	27
Fuji 100 Acros	EI 100/21	12.30	–	–	6.45	–	–	–	–	–
Fuji Neopan 400	EI 400/27	10	14	20	7.30	9.30	15	4.30	6.45	9
	EI 800/30	–	–	–	8.45	–	–	5.45	–	–
	EI 1600/33	–	–	–	13.30	–	–	8.30	–	–
	EI 3200/36	–	–	–	–	–	–	–	–	–
Fuji Neopan 1600	EI 400/27	–	–	–	–	–	–	–	–	–
	EI 800/30	–	–	–	4.3	–	–	–	–	–
	EI 1600/33	–	–	–	6.3	10	15	3.30	–	–
	EI 3200/36	–	–	–	–	–	–	5.45	–	–

The development times for other manufacturers' films are a general guide. The specification of these products may have changed over time and as a result these development times may need to be adjusted. If necessary the given times should be adjusted to give the result required.

Darkroom Data Guide

Stop, Fix, Wash and Rinse

After developing a film it is essential to use a stop bath to arrest the developer action and to follow this with adequate fixing and washing. A final rinse then ensures mark free film drying.

For best results it is recommended that all process solutions are kept at the same temperature or at least within 5ºC (9ºF) of the developer temperature.

Stop Bath

When using "one-shot" processing in small spiral tanks a water rinse can substitute for a stop bath. After development film can be rinsed in water but we recommend that an acid stop bath is used such as ILFORD ILFOSTOP (with indicator dye) or ILFOSTOP PRO (without indicator dye).

When deep tanks or dishes (trays) of process solutions are in use a stop bath immediately stops development and reduces carry over of excess developer into the fixer bath. This helps to maintain the activity and prolong the life of the fixer solution.

ILFORD Stop Bath	ILFOSTOP	ILFOSTOP PRO
Dilution	1+19	1+19
Temperature range	18–24 ºC (64–75ºF)	18–24 ºC (64–75ºF)
Time (seconds) at 20ºC (68ºF)	10	10
Capacity - films/litre (unreplenished)	15 x 135–36	22 x 135–36

The process time given for the stop bath is the minimum required. if necessary a longer time may be used and should not cause any process problems provided it is not excessive.

Fixing

The recommended fixers ILFORD RAPID FIXER and ILFORD HYPAM liquid fixers and ILFORD ILFOFIX II powder fixer, are non-hardening fixers.

Kodak Professional D-76 Developer

KODAK PROFESSIONAL D-76 Developer provides full emulsion speed and excellent shadow detail with normal contrast, and produces fine grain with a variety of continuous-tone black-and-white films. For greater sharpness, but with a slight increase in graininess, you can use a 1:1 dilution of this developer. It yields a long density range, and its development latitude allows push processing with relatively low fog.

Proper replenishment of D-76 Developer with KODAK PROFESSIONAL D-76R Replenisher will increase the capacity of the developer and maintain process consistency without an increase in the development time.

Agitation

Proper agitation is very important for consistent and uniform results. Agitation helps remove the by-products of development from the surface of the film so that fresh developer can act on the exposed silver halide in the emulsion. Because agitation affects the rate of development, particularly in high-density areas, you can achieve consistent negative quality only if agitation is uniform over the whole surface of the film, and when the degree of agitation is similar for each film or batch of films.

Agitation should always consist of irregular or random movements that will not cause solution currents to flow over the film constantly in any one direction; these currents increase film density along their paths, causing non-uniformity.

Agitating Rolls in a small tank

The times given for small-tank processing are based on the following agitation procedure:

1. Fill the empty tank with developer.

2. Start the timer. In the dark, carefully place the loaded reel into the developer solution.

3. Quickly attach the top to the tank. Firmly tap the bottom of the tank against the work surface from a height of approximately 2.5 cm (1 inch) to dislodge air bubbles from the surface of the film. Air bubbles can interfere with development and produce low-density circles on the film.

4. Provide initial agitation of up to 5 cycles, depending on your results. For KODAK PROFESSIONAL T-MAX Films, provide initial agitation of 5 to 7 cycles in 5 seconds. For an invertible tank, one cycle consists of

Darkroom Data Guide

rotating the tank upside down and then back to the upright position. For a noninvertible tank, one cycle consists of sliding the tank back and forth over a 25.4 cm (10-inch) distance. With tanks that have a handle for turning the reel, rotate the reel back and forth gently through about one-half turn at a rate of one cycle per second during the agitation intervals. Steps 2 through 4 will take approximately 7 to 20 seconds, depending on the type of tank.

5. Let the tank sit for the remainder of the first 30 seconds.

6. After the first 30 seconds, agitate for 5 seconds at 30-second intervals. Agitation should consist of 2 to5 cycles, depending on the contrast you need and the type of tank.

Development Times

The development times in the following tables are starting-point recommendations; for critical applications, run tests to determine the best development time. If your films are consistently too low in contrast, increase the development time slightly (10 to 15 percent); if they are too contrasty, decrease the development time slightly (10 to 15 percent).

If you use D-76 Developer diluted 1:1, dilute it just before you use it, and discard it after processing the batch of film.

Before using the diluted developer, make certain that there are no air bubbles in the solution. If air is coming out of the solution and forming bubbles, let the solution stand until the bubbles dissipate.

Don't reuse or replenish the diluted solution. You can develop one 135-3 roll (80 square inches) in 473 ml (16 ounces) or two rolls together in 946 ml (one quart) of diluted developer.

If you process one 135-36 roll in a 237 ml (8-ounce) tank or two 135-36 rolls in a 473 ml (16-ounce) tank, increase the development time by 10 percent (see the following tables).

KODAK PROFESSIONAL D-76 Developer (Full Strength)

KODAK Film	Small Tank*					Large Tank†				
	18°C (65°F)	20°C (68°F)	21°C (70°F)	22°C (72°F)	24°C (75°F)	18°C (65°F)	20°C (68°F)	21°C (70°F)	22°C (72°F)	24°C (75°F)
T-MAX 100 Professional	10 ½	9	8	7	6	11 ½	10	9	8	6 ½
PROFESSIONAL T-MAX 100	7 ½	6 ½	5 ½	5	4 ¼	8 ¼	7 ¼	6 ½	5 ¾	4 ¾
T-MAX 400 Professional and PROFESSIONAL T-MAX 400	9	8	7	6 ½	5 ½	10	9	8	7 ½	6 ½
T-MAX P3200 Professional	See the table below					See the table below				
VERICHROME Pan	8	7	5 ½	5	4 ½	9	8	7	6	5
PLUS-X Pan / PX PLUS-X Pan Professional / PXP	6 ½	5 ½	5	4 ½	3 ¾	7 ½	6 ½	6	5 ½	4 ½
PROFESSIONAL PLUS-X 125	6 ½	5 ½	5	4 ½	4	7 ¼	6 ¼	5 ¾	5 ¼	4 ½
TRI-X Pan	9	8	7 ½	6 ½	5 ½	10	9	8	7	6
TRI-X Pan Professional	9	8	7 ½	7	6	10	9	8 ½	8	7
PROFESSIONAL TRI-X 400 Film / 400TX	8	6 ¾	6 ¼	5 ½	4 ¾	9 ¼	7 ¾	7	6 ½	5 ½
PROFESSIONAL TRI-X 320 Film / 320TXP	10	9	8 ¼	7 ½	6 ½	11 ½	10 ¼	9 ½	8 ¾	7 ½
High Speed Infrared	9 ½	8 ½	7 ½	7	6	10	9	8	7 ½	6 ½

* With agitation at 30-second intervals.
† With agitation at 1-minute intervals.
Note: Tank development times shorter than 5 minutes may produce poor uniformity.

KODAK T-MAX P3200 Professional Film in KODAK PROFESSIONAL D-76 Developer (Full Strength)

Exposed at EI	Small Tank*				
	20°C (68°F)	21°C (70°F)	24°C (75°F)	27°C (80°F)	29°C (85°F)
400/27*	10 ½	9 ½	7 ½	6	4 ½
800/30*	11	10	8	6 ½	5
1600/33*	11 ½	10 ½	8 ½	7	5 ½
3200/36*	15	13 ½	11	8 ½	7 ½
6400/39*	17 ½	16	12 ½	10 ½	9

* With agitation at 30-second intervals.
Note: Tank development times shorter than 5 minutes may produce poor uniformity.

KODAK PROFESSIONAL T-MAX P3200 Film in KODAK PROFESSIONAL D-76 Developer (Full Strength)

Exposed at EI	Small Tank*				
	20°C (68°F)	21°C (70°F)	24°C (75°F)	27°C (80°F)	29°C (85°F)
400/27*	10 ½	9 ½	7 ½	6	5
800/30*	11 ½	10 ½	8 ½	6 ½	5 ½
1600/33*	12 ½	11 ½	9	7 ½	6
3200/36*	14	13	10 ½	8 ½	6 ½
6400/39*	15 ½	14	11 ½	9	7 ½

* With agitation at 30-second intervals.
Note: Tank development times shorter than 5 minutes may produce poor uniformity.

KODAK PROFESSIONAL D-76 Developer (1:1)

KODAK Film	Development Times (Minutes)									
	Small Tank*					Large Tank†				
	18°C (65°F)	20°C (68°F)	21°C (70°F)	22°C (72°F)	24°C (75°F)	18°C (65°F)	20°C (68°F)	21°C (70°F)	22°C (72°F)	24°C (75°F)
T-MAX 100 Professional	14 ½	12	11	10	8 ½	—	—	—	—	—
PROFESSIONAL T-MAX 100	11	9 ½	8 ½	7 ½	6 ¼	—	—	—	—	—
T-MAX 400 Professional and PROFESSIONAL T-MAX 400	14 ½	12 ½	11	10	9	—	—	—	—	—
VERICHROME Pan	11	9	8	7	6	12 ½	10	9	8	7
PLUS-X Pan PLUS-X Pan Professional	8	7	6 ½	6	5	10	9	8	7 ½	7
PROFESSIONAL PLUS-X 125	10	8 ½	7 ¾	7 ¼	6	11 ¼	9 ¾	8 ¾	8	6 ¾
TRI-X Pan	11	10	9 ½	9	8	13	12	11	10	9
PROFESSIONAL TRI-X 400 Film / 400TX	10 ¾	9 ¾	9	8 ½	7 ¾	12 ¼	11	10 ½	9 ¾	8 ¾
PROFESSIONAL TRI-X 320 Film / 320TXP	14 ¼	12 ¾	11 ¾	10 ¾	9 ¼	—	—	—	—	—

* With agitation at 30-second intervals.
† With agitation at 1-minute intervals.

Sheet Films

KODAK PROFESSIONAL D-76 Developer (Full Strength)

KODAK Sheet Film	Development Times (Minutes)									
	Tray*					Large Tank†				
	18°C (65°F)	20°C (68°F)	21°C (70°F)	22°C (72°F)	24°C (75°F)	18°C (65°F)	20°C (68°F)	21°C (70°F)	22°C (72°F)	24°C (75°F)
T-MAX 100 Professional	9 ½	7	6 ½	5 ½	5	11 ½	9 ½	8 ½	7 ½	7
PROFESSIONAL T-MAX 100	6 ¾	5 ¾	5 ¼	4 ¾	4	8 ¼	7 ¼	6 ½	5 ¾	4 ¾
T-MAX 400 Professional and PROFESSIONAL T-MAX 400	9 ½	7	6 ½	6	5 ½	11	10	9	8	7
TRI-X Pan Professional / TXT	6	5 ½	5	5	4 ½	7 ½	7	6 ½	6	5 ½
PROFESSIONAL TRI-X 320 Film / 320TXP	6 ¾	6	5 ½	5	4 ½	8 ½	7 ½	7	6 ¼	5 ½
PLUS-X Pan Professional / PXT	7	6	5 ½	5	4 ½	9	8	7 ½	7	6
EKTAPAN	9	8	7	6 ½	5 ½	11	10	9	8 ½	7 ½
High Speed Infrared / HSI	11	9 ½	8 ½	7 ½	6 ½	10	9	8	7 ½	6 ½

* With continuous agitation.
† With agitation at 1-minute intervals.

Processing "Pushed" Roll Films in a Small Tank

Use the development times in the table below to process roll films exposed at speeds higher than their normal ISO or EI ratings. When you expose the film listed in the table at a speed 1 stop faster than the rated speed, we recommend that you develop them for the normal time.

The underexposure latitude of these films is wide enough to give you good results with finer grain than you would obtain with push processing.

Darkroom Data Guide

KODAK PROFESSIONAL D-76 Developer (Full Strength)

KODAK Roll Film	Development Times (Minutes)			
	20°C (68°F)	24°C (75°F)	20°C (68°F)	24°C (75°F)
	EI 200 (Normal Processing)		EI 400 (2-Stop Push Processing)	
T-MAX 100 Professional	9	6	11	7 ½
PROFESSIONAL T-MAX 100	6 ½	4 ¼	8 ¼	5 ½
	EI 800 (Normal Processing)		EI 1600 (2-Stop Push Processing)	
T-MAX 400 Professional and PROFESSIONAL T-MAX 400	8	5 ½	10 ½	7
TRI-X Pan	8	5 ½	13	10
PROFESSIONAL TRI-X 400 Film / 400TX	8	4 ¾	9 ½	6 ½

Small Tank Processing, Intermittent Agitation for Tanks That Can Be Inverted

ROLL FILMS

KODAK Film	Film Code	Development Time (Minutes)				Comments	Reference Publication
		20°C (68°F)			24°C (75°F)		
		KODAK PROFESSIONAL XTOL Developer	KODAK PROFESSIONAL Developer D-76	KODAK PROFESSIONAL HC-110 Developer (Dilution B)	KODAK PROFESSIONAL T-MAX Developer (1:4)		
KODAK PROFESSIONAL T-MAX 100 New	100TMX	7 1/2	6 1/2	6	6 1/4		F-4016
T-MAX 100 Professional	TMX	6 3/4	9	7	6 1/2	Also T-MAX Developer (1:7) for 10 minutes or (1:9) for 14 minutes at 24°C (75°F)	F-32
KODAK PROFESSIONAL T-MAX 400 New	400TMY	6 1/2	8	6	6	Packaging change only. No change to processing time	F-4016
T-MAX 400 Professional	TMY	6 1/2	8	6	6	Also T-MAX Developer (1:7) for 10 minutes or (1:9) for 15 minutes at 24°C (75°F)	F-32
KODAK PROFESSIONAL T-MAX P3200 New	EI 400	9 1/2	10 1/2	7 1/2	6 1/2		F-4016
	EI 800	10 1/2	11 1/2	8 1/2	7 1/2		
	EI 1600	11 1/2	12 1/2	9 1/4	8		
	EI 3200 (P3200TMZ)	13 1/2	14	10 1/2	9 1/2		
	EI 6400	15 1/4	15 1/2	12	11		
	EI 12,500	17 1/4	—	—	12		
	EI 25,000	19	—	—	13 1/2		
T-MAX P3200 Professional	EI 400	7 1/2	10 1/2	7 1/2	6		F-32
	EI 800	8 1/4	11	8	6 1/2	Also T-MAX Developer (1:7) for 12 1/2 minutes or (1:9) for 15 minutes at 24°C (75°F)	
	EI 1600 (TMZ)	9 1/4	11 1/2	9	7		
	EI 3200	11	15	11 1/2	9 1/2	—	
	EI 6400	12 1/2	17 1/2	14	11	—	
	EI 12,500	15 1/4	—	—	12	—	
	EI 25,000	18 1/2	—	—	14	—	
KODAK PROFESSIONAL PLUS-X 125 New	125PX	(135) 5 1/2 (120/220) 6	5 1/2	3 1/2	4 1/4		F-4018
PLUS-X Pan	PX	5 1/4	5 1/2	5	5	Also Developer D-76 (1:1) for 7 minutes at 20°C (68°F)	F-8

PLUS-X Pan Professional		PXP	5 1/2	5 1/2	5	5	Also Developer D-76 (1:1) for 7 minutes at 20°C (68°F)	
KODAK PROFESSIONAL TRI-X 320	New	320TXP	7 3/4	9	4 3/4	5 1/4	Also T-MAX Developer for 7 1/4 minutes at 20°C (68°F)	F-4017
TRI-X Pan Professional		TXP	6 1/4	8	5 1/2	6 1/2	Also KODAK PROFESSIONAL Developer DK-50 (1:1) for 8 minutes at 20°C (68°F)	F-9
KODAK PROFESSIONAL TRI-X 400	New	400TX	7	6 3/4	3 3/4	4 3/4	Also Developer D-76 (1:1) for 9 3/4 minutes at 20°C (68°F)	F-4017
TRI-X Pan		TX	(135) 6 3/4 (120) 6 1/4	8	7 1/2	5 1/2	Also Developer DK-50 (1:1) for 8 minutes at 20°C (68°F)	F-9
VERICHROME Pan			6	7	5	4	Also Developer D-76 (1:1) for 9 minutes at 20°C (68°F)	F-7

Kodak Developers

KODAK PROFESSIONAL HC-110 Developer

KODAK PROFESSIONAL HC-110 Developer is a highly concentrated liquid developer. It is intended for use with a variety of black-and-white films, some graphic-arts films and some glass plates.

It can be used for replenished and non-replenished systems. Use KODAK PROFESSIONAL HC-110 Developer Replenisher to replenish.

Main Features

- Highly active • Short development times
- Liquid concentrate
- Easy mixing
- Clean solution
- Cleaner tanks, racks, and reels; less equipment maintenance
- Long solution life • Fewer chemical dumps; less waste
- Stable solutions • Easy process control, even with low utilization
- Quality of stock solutions maintained over a long time
- Good shelf life

Preparing working solutions

You can prepare HC-110 Developer working solutions by diluting stock solution or concentrate. (Both mixing methods provide the same photographic characteristics.)

To prepare stock solution, dilute one part concentrate with three parts water. To prepare working solutions, dilute stock solution or concentrate according to the following tables. Mix either stock or working solutions at a temperature between 10 and 32°C (50 and 90°F).

Take care when measuring the concentrate, because of its viscosity. Follow these recommendations for handling.

- Pour the concentrate slowly to avoid air bubbles. If air bubbles form, wait for them to dissipate before measuring the concentrate.

Wait for the concentrate to run down the sides of the measuring container. (The concentrate will adhere to the sides of a graduated cylinder.)

- When measuring small amounts of concentrate, use a graduated cylinder accurate to 0.5 millilitre. (To simplify measuring small amounts, use a positive-displacement method such as a syringe.)

98

Rinse the measuring container with water at least five times, and pour each rinse into the mixing container. This ensures that all the concentrate is dissolved in the water.

• Mix the solution for several minutes until the concentrate is fully dissolved.
Caution

KODAK PROFESSIONAL HC-110 Developer is a highly concentrated liquid that you must dilute before use. The following tables provide dilution instructions on preparing working solutions from either stock solution or concentrate.

Exercise caution when following the mixing instructions in the tables, being certain not to intermingle their data.

PREPARING WORKING SOLUTIONS FROM STOCK SOLUTION*				
To Mix Working Solution		Add This Amount of Stock Solution†	To This Amount of Water†	Ratio of Stock Solution to Water
Dilution	Amount			
A	300 mL	75 mL	225 mL	1:3
	500 mL	125 mL	375 mL	
	1 qt	236 mL (8 fl oz)	708 mL (24 fl oz)	
	1 L	250 mL	750 mL	
	5 L	1.25 L	3.75 L	
	7.6 L (2 gal)	1.9 L (2 qt)	5.7 L (6 qt)	
	18.9 L (5 gal)	4.73 L (5 qt)	14.17 L (15 qt)	
B	300 mL	38 mL	262 mL	1:7
	500 mL	63 mL	437 mL	
	1 qt	118 mL (4 fl oz)	826 mL (28 fl oz)	
	1 L	125 mL	875 mL	
	5 L	625 mL	4.38 mL	
	7.6 L (2 gal)	950 mL (1 qt)	6.65 L (7 qt)	
	18.9 L (5 gal)	2.36 L (2.5 qt)	16.54 L (17.5 qt)	
C	7.6 L (2 gal)	1.54 L (52 fl oz)	6.08 L (6 qt 13 fl oz)	1:4
	18.9 L (5 gal)	3.78 L (4 qt)	15.12 L (16 qt)	
D	7.6 L (2 gal)	770 mL (26 fl oz)	6.84 L (7 qt 6 fl oz)	1:9
	18.9 L (5 gal)	1.89 L (2 qt)	17.01 L (18 qt)	
E	7.6 L (2 gal)	630 mL (21 fl oz)	6.97 L (7 qt 11 fl oz)	1:11
	18.9 L (5 gal)	1.58 L (1 qt 11 fl oz)	17.32 L (18 qt 21 fl oz)	
F	7.6 L (2 gal)	380 mL (13 fl oz)	7.22 L (7 qt 19 fl oz)	1:19
	18.9 L (5 gal)	950 mL (1 qt)	17.95 L (19 qt)	

* IMPORTANT NOTE: Due to the high viscosity of the developer concentrate, it is preferable to dilute it to a *stock solution*.
This may be a more convenient way to store the chemical for future preparation into a *working solution*, per the above instructions.
† Due to rounding of decimals, slight variations occur when amounts are given in millilitres and fluid ounces.

	Development Time (Minutes)									
KODAK Film	Small Tank* Manual Agitation at 30-Second Intervals					Large Tank† Manual Agitation at 1-Minute Intervals				
	18°C (65°F)	20°C (68°F)	21°C (70°F)	22°C (72°F)	24°F (75°F)	18°C (65°F)	20°C (68°F)	21°C (70°F)	22°C (72°F)	24°F (75°F)
DILUTION A										
Recording 2475	5½	4½	4	3½	3	NR				
TRI-X Pan / TX	4¼	3¾	3¼	3	2½	4¾	4¼	4	3¾	3¼
TRI-X Pan Professional / TXP	NR					3½	3	3	2¾	2¼
DILUTION B										
PLUS-X Pan / PX PLUS-X Pan Professional / PXP‡	6	5	4½	4	3½	6½	5½	5	4¾	4
PROFESSIONAL PLUS-X 125	4	3½	3	2¾	2½	4½	3¾	3½	3¼	2¾
Recording 2475	11	9	8	7	6	NR				
Technical Pan / TP	For information on developing KODAK Technical Pan Films to varying contrast indexes for specific applications, see KODAK Publication No. P-255, KODAK Technical Pan Films.									
T-MAX 100 Professional / TMX	8	7	6½	6	5	8½	7½	7	6½	5½
PROFESSIONAL T-MAX 100	6½	6	5½	5	4	7½	6½	6	5¼	4½
T-MAX 400 Professional and PROFESSIONAL T-MAX 400	6½	6	5½	5	4½	8	7	6½	6	5
T-MAX P3200 Professional / TMZ PROFESSIONAL T-MAX P3200	See the tables below.									
TRI-X Pan / TX	8½	7½	6½	6	5	9½	8½	8	7½	6½
TRI-X Pan Professional / TXP	5¾	5½	5¼	4¾	3¾	7	6¼	6	5½	5
PROFFESSIONAL TRI-X 400 Film / 400TX	4½	3¾	3½	3	2½	5	4½	4	3½	3
PROFESSIONAL TRI-X 320 Film / 320TXP	5¼	4¾	4¼	4	3½	6¼	5½	5	4½	4
VERICHROME Pan / VP	6	5	4½	4	2	8	6½	6	5½	4½

* Development on a reel in a small roll-film tank.
† Development of several reels in a basket.
‡ Development times also apply to tank development using gaseous-burst agitation. Set the burst duration for 1 second with 10 seconds between bursts; provide sufficient pressure to increase the solution level 16 mm (⅝ inch).
NR = Not recommended

Note: Tank-development times shorter than 5 minutes may produce unsatisfactory uniformity.

Kodak T- Max Developer

KODAK PROFESSIONAL T-MAX Developer is a moderately active, liquid black-and-white film developer that offers enhanced shadow detail in normally processed and push-processed films. The same description applies to KODAK PROFESSIONAL T-MAX RS Developer and Replenisher except that it is a black-and-white film developer and replenisher. Like T-MAX Developer, T-MAX RS Developer and Replenisher produces higher image quality (enhanced shadow detail) than current push-processing developers when you process film normally or push it one, two, or three stops.

You can use T-MAX Developer to process roll sizes of KODAK PROFESSIONAL T-MAX Films and most other black-and-white continuous-tone films. Do not use this developer to process sheet film. You can use T-MAX RS Developer and Replenisher to process all roll and sheet sizes of KODAK PROFESSIONAL T-MAX Films, as well as most other black-and-white continuous-tone films.

T-MAX Developer is intended for use in unreplenished systems. For replenished systems, use T-MAX RS Developer and Replenisher. T-MAX RS Developer and Replenisher is a hydroquinone-based, two-part developer specially formulated for replenished systems, but you can also use it in unreplenished systems.

T-MAX Developer is available as a one-part concentrate in sizes to make one gallon and five gallons of working solution. You can easily mix smaller volumes by mixing one part of the concentrate with four parts water. T-MAX RS Developer and Replenisher is available in convenient sizes to make one gallon and ten gallons of solution; use this solution as a working-tank solution or a replenisher. The ten-gallon size consists of two separate units, each to make five gallons of solution.

Manual Processing

Small-Tank Processing   (8- or 16-ounce tank)—Rolls

Agitate once every 30 seconds. Drop the loaded film reel into the developer and attach the top to the tank. Firmly tap the tank on the top of the work surface to dislodge any air bubbles. Provide initial agitation of 5 to 7 inversion cycles in 5 seconds, i.e. extend your arm and vigorously twist your wrist 180 degrees as shown below.

Then repeat this agitation procedure at 30-second intervals for the rest of the development time.

KODAK T-MAX RS Developer and Replenisher								
KODAK Film	**Speed Rating**	**Development Time (Minutes)**						
	EI	18°C (65°F)	20°C (68°F)	21°C (70°F)	22°C (72°F)	24°C (75°F)	27°C (80°F)	29°C (85°F)
T-MAX 100 Professional	100/200	NR	8	7	7	6	—	—
	400	—	12	11	10	9	—	—
	800	—	NR	NR	NR	11 ½	—	—
PROFESSIONAL T-MAX 100	100/200	NR	8	7 ½	7	6 ¼	—	—
	400	—	12 ¼	—	—	10	—	—
	800	—	—	—	—	11 ¾	—	—
T-MAX 400 Professional and PROFESSIONAL T-MAX 400	400/800	NR	7	6	6	5	—	—
	1600	—	10	9	8	7	—	—
	3200	—	13	12	11	9 ½	—	—
T-MAX P3200 Professional	400*	—	8	7	6 ½	6	5 ½	5
	800	—	9	8 ½	7 ½	6 ½	6	5 ½
	1600	—	10 ½	9 ½	8 ½	7 ½	7	6
	3200	—	13	12	11	10	9	8
	6400	—	15	14	13	11	10	9
	12,500*	—	18	16	14	12	11	10
	25,000*	—	NR	NR	16	14	13	11
PROFESSIONAL T-MAX P3200	400*	—	9	8 ½	7 ½	7	6 ½	5 ½
	800	—	10 ½	9 ½	9	8 ½	7 ½	6 ½
	1600	—	12	11	10	9 ½	8 ½	7
	3200	—	14 ½	13	12	11 ½	10	8 ½
	6400	—	16 ½	15	13 ½	13	11 ½	10
	12,500*	—	18 ½	17	15 ½	14 ½	13	11
	25,000*	—	NR	NR	17	16 ½	14 ½	12 ½
PLUS-X Pan	125/250	6 ½	5 ½	4 ½†	4†	3 ½†	—	—
PLUS-X Pan Professional	500	NR	9	8 ½	7 ½	6 ½	—	—
PROFESSIONAL PLUS-X 125	125/250	5	4 ¼†	4†	3 ½†	3†	—	—
	500	—	7 ¼	6 ½	6	5	—	—
TRI-X Pan	400/800	7	6	5 ½	5 ½	5	—	—
	1600	—	9 ½	9	8 ½	8	—	—
	3200	—	12	11 ½	11 ½	11	—	—
TRI-X Pan Professional	320	5	4†	3 ½†	3 ½†	3†	—	—
PROFESSIONAL TRI-X 400 Film / 400TX	400/800	4 ¾†	4 ½†	4 ¼†	4†	3 ½†	—	—
	1600	8 ½	7 ¾	7 ¼	6 ¾	6	—	—
	3200	—	9 ½	9	8 ¼	7 ½	—	—
PROFESSIONAL TRI-X 320 Film / 320TXP	320	4 ½†	4†	3 ½†	3 ¼†	2 ¾†	—	—
VERICHROME Pan	125	—	4†	4†	3 ½†	3 ½†	—	—

*Make tests to determine if results at these ratings are acceptable for your needs.
†Development times shorter than 5 minutes may produce unsatisfactory uniformity.

NR = Not recommended
Note: The development times in bold type are suggested starting points.

ILFORD

January 2004

FACT SHEET

B&W PAPER DEVELOPERS

DEVELOPERS FOR THE DISH/TRAY PROCESSING OF BLACK AND WHITE PHOTOGRAPHIC PAPERS

ILFORD MULTIGRADE developer

MULTIGRADE is a rapid liquid concentrate dimezone-s/hydroquinone developer suitable for the dish/tray developing of all black and white photographic papers both resin coated, RC, and traditional fibre based, FB ones. It is usually used at a dilution of 1+9 but for greater development control and economy it can be used at 1+14. MULTIGRADE developer is clean working, has excellent keeping properties and gives a neutral image tone with most papers. MULTIGRADE developer is designed for use at ambient room temperatures, nominally 20°C/68°F. We do not recommend its use for high temperature or machine processing applications. It is not suitable for developing films.

ILFORD PQ UNIVERSAL developer

PQ UNIVERSAL is a liquid concentrate dimezone-s/hydroquinone developer suitable for the dish/tray developing of all RC and FB black and white photographic papers. Used at a dilution of 1+9 it is clean working and has excellent keeping properties. It gives a slightly warm of neutral image tone with most papers.

In addition PQ UNIVERSAL can be used to dish/tray process ILFORD and some other technical films. It is also suitable for dish/tray developing of general purpose sheet films when a fast working, high contrast developer is needed and a high degree of enlargement is not required. For film processing applications it is diluted either 1+9 (high contrast) or 1+19 (pictorial contrast). PQ UNIVERSAL is not recommended for processing general purpose 35mm and roll film formats.

PQ UNIVERSAL developer is designed for use at ambient room temperatures, nominally 20°C/68°F. We do not recommend its use for high temperature or machine processing applications

ILFORD BROMOPHEN developer

BROMOPHEN is a phenidone/hydroquinone developer supplied in powder form. It is suitable for dish/tray developing all RC and FB black and white photographic papers. It is made into a stock solution that is diluted 1+3 for use. It is economical, clean working and has good keeping properties. It gives a slightly warm of neutral image tone with most papers. It is particularly recommended for dish/tray developing MULTIGRADE Warmtone RC and FB papers to get the warmest image tone.

BROMOPHEN developer is designed for use at ambient room temperatures, nominally 20°C/68°F. We do not recommend its use for high temperature or machine processing applications. It is not suitable for developing films.

Mixing instructions

Note Photographic chemicals are not hazardous when used correctly. It is recommended that gloves, eye protection and an apron or overall are worn when handling and mixing all chemicals. Always follow the specific health and safety recommendations on the chemical packaging. Photochemical material safety data sheets containing full details for the safe handling, disposal and transportation of ILFORD chemicals are available from ILFORD agents or directly from the ILFORD web site at **www.ilford.com**.

B&W PAPER DEVELOPERS

Preparing MULTIGRADE and PQ UNIVERSAL developer

MULTIGRADE and PQ UNIVERSAL liquid concentrates are mixed with water for use. MULTIGRADE can be used at a dilution of either 1+9 or 1+14. PQ UNIVERSAL is used at a dilution of 1+9 for paper or 1+9/1+19 for technical films and sheet films.

Prepare the working strength solutions of MULTIGRADE and PQ UNIVERSAL developers directly before they are needed. Determine the amount of solution needed for the processing session, making sure that it is a least enough to fill the developing dish/tray to a depth of about half full. Measure out the appropriate amount of concentrate using the smallest measuring cylinder appropriate to the liquid volume: it is easier and more accurate to measure 100 ml of solution in a 100 ml cylinder than a 1000 ml cylinder.

Add the concentrate to the mixing vessel. A large measuring jug is a good mixing vessel as it provides a check on the total quantity of solution mixed. Using an appropriately sized measuring cylinder, measure out the required dilution water using hot and cold water to get to the solution's working temperature, 20°C/68°F. Rinse out the measuring cylinder used for the concentrate into the mixing vessel with some of the dilution water. Finally add the remainder of the dilution water to make up to the final working volume and stir the solution thoroughly. The developer is then ready to use.

Preparing BROMOPHEN stock developer

BROMOPHEN cartons contain two parts, A and B that must be dissolved in water for use. Always make up the developer stock solution to the volume stated on the carton, do not attempt to prepare smaller solution quantities by using fractional parts of each powder, however larger stock solution quantities can be prepared by using multiples of whole packs.

To prepare stock developer, dissolve the contents of part A (the smaller bag) in about three-quarters of the total solution volume (see carton) of warm water at about 40°C/104°F. Stir until most of the part A powder has dissolved, continue to stir while gradually adding the contents of part B (the larger bag). Keep stirring until no more powder dissolves. NB, it is normal for a few grains of powder to remain un-dissolved. Add cold water to make up to the final volume (see carton) and stir. Allow to cool to room temperature, nominally 20°C/68°F. Store in a tightly capped bottle until needed for use.

Preparing working strength BROMOPHEN.

To use BROMOPHEN the stock solution is diluted 1+3 with water to make a working strength solution. Prepare the working strength solution from the stock solution directly before it is needed. Treat the BROMOPHEN stock solution as if it were a liquid concentrate and use the mixing method and information given above in the section called "Preparing MULTIGRADE and PQ UNIVERSAL developer".

As most water drawn from pressure mains is highly aerated, we advise that users draw off the water they need and leave it to stand for a few minutes before using it to make up developers.

Thoroughly wash all utensils, measuring and mixing vessels after use. Do not contaminate developer solutions with either stop bath or fixer solutions.

pH and specific gravity

The following table gives the pH and specific gravity (SG) for fresh solutions of MULTIGRADE, PQ UNIVERSAL and BROMOPHEN developers. These figures were obtained under carefully controlled laboratory conditions and may differ slightly from measurements made by users in their own working areas. Users should make their own control measurements from their own accurately mixed fresh solutions for later comparison. Ideally a pH meter should be used to measure solution pH but if one is not available pH measurement sticks can be used. These are available in various pH ranges and those covering a range from pH 7 to pH 10 are sufficient. SG can be measured by using a hydrometer and one covering the range from 1.000 to 1.200 is useful for a wide range of photographic process solutions.

Developer	dilution	pH	SG at 20°C
MULTIGRADE	1+9	10.45–10.55	1.022
	1+14		1.011
PQ UNIVERSAL	1+9	10.48– 10.58	1.022
	1+19		1.011
BROMOPHEN	stock	10.30–10.50	1.106
	1+3		1.025

PROCESSING PAPER
Dish/tray processing

MULTIGRADE, PQ UNIVERSAL and BROMOPHEN working strength developer solutions should be used in a dish/tray at ambient room temperature. The recommended developing temperature is 20°C (68°F) ±1°C (2°F). Slightly lower temperatures can be used but development would need to be extended slightly. Slightly higher temperatures can also be used but development times would need to be reduced. These developers are not designed for high temperature processing. High temperatures will reduce the effective solution life considerably and may give very short development times that can lead to uneven processing being seen.

Darkroom Data Guide

B&W PAPER DEVELOPERS

Before starting to process prepare the require volume of all the process solutions according to dish/tray size used and number of sheets of paper to be processed. The solution volume should be enough to fill the processing dish/tray to a depth of about half full, it must be enough to cover the paper completely during processing. Check the temperatures of all the process solutions and adjust them to be ± 1°C (2°F) of the temperature being used.

When dish/tray processing intermittent agitation is used. For a single sheet immerse the paper completely in the developer and gently rock the dish from side to side taking care to avoid any spillage. This method of agitation is used for all subsequent processing steps.

When developing multiple sheets of paper at once, intermittent agitation is given by interleaving them. To interleave paper, slip the sheets into the solution one at a time, emulsion side down. When all the sheets are in the solution, pull the sheet from the bottom and place it on the top of the pile of sheets in the dish/tray. Continue this process of moving the bottom sheet to the top until the process time is complete. Use this method of agitation for all subsequent processing steps.

The number of sheets that can be interleaved at one time is up to the individual, however do take care as too many sheets with too little agitation can lead to uneven processing. FB papers are more difficult to interleave than the waterproof RC based papers that remain rigid when wet. The traditional FB papers absorb far more liquid than RC ones and when they are wet they go rather limp and without careful handling they are more prone to damage.

Remove the paper(s) from the dish/tray 10 seconds before the end of the development time and allow developer to drain before placing it the stop bath.

Development times
RC paper

ILFORD developer	Dilution	°C/°F	Time (min:sec)
Liquids			
MULTIGRADE	1+9	20/68	1:00
MULTIGRADE	1+14	20/68	1:30
PQ UNIVERSAL	1+9	20/68	2:00
Powder			
BROMOPHEN	1+3	20/68	2:00

Approximately double these times are recommended with MULTIGRADE RC COOLTONE paper to obtain the coolest image colour – see the MULTIGRADE RC COOLTONE fact sheet.

FB paper

ILFORD developer	Dilution	°C/°F	Time (min) Recommended	Range
Liquids				
MULTIGRADE	1+9	20/68	2	1½–3
	1+14	20/68	3	2–5
PQ UNIVERSAL	1+9	20/68	2	1½–3
Powder				
BROMOPHEN	1+3	20/68	2	1½–3

On correctly exposed FB prints, the image will begin to appear after 35 seconds with these developers. Development may be extended to 6 minutes without any noticeable change in contrast or fog.

To maintain print to print consistency when batch processing a large number of either RC or FB prints, it may be advantageous to reduce exposure slightly and extend development.

Developer capacities
The following table gives the developing capacity of 1 litre of working strength developer.

ILFORD developer	Dilution	20·3x25·4cm (8x10 inch) ILFORD prints RC paper	20·3x25·4cm (8x10 inch) ILFORD prints FB paper
Liquids			
MULTIGRADE	1+9	100	50
MULTIGRADE	1+14	70	40
PQ UNIVERSAL	1+9	70	45
Powder			
BROMOPHEN	1+3	70	45

Approximately half these capacities are achieved if only MULTIGRADE RC COOLTONE is processed. This is because of the longer development times recommended with MULTIGRADE RC COOLTONE paper.

Stop

ILFORD stop bath	Dilution	°C/°F	Time (sec)
Liquid			
ILFOSTOP	1+19	18–24/64–75	10
ILFOSTOP PRO	1+19	18–24/64–75	10

Fix

ILFORD non-hardening FIXER	Dilution	°C/°F	RC time (min)	FB time (min)
Liquids				
ILFORD RAPID	1+4	18–24/64–75	½	1
FIXER	1+9	18–24/64–75	1	2
HYPAM	1+4	18–24/64–75	½	1
	1+9	18–24/64–75	1	2
Powder				
ILFOFIX II	stock	18–24/64–75	2	3

B&W PAPER DEVELOPERS

Washing RC paper

	Temperature (°C/°F)	Time (sec)
Fresh, running water	Above 5/41	120

When it is important to obtain a print in the shortest possible time, vigorously wash ILFORD resin coated papers for 30 seconds in running water.

Prolonged immersion in water can cause edge penetration and print curl with resin coated papers: for this reason, avoid wet times longer than 15 minutes.

Washing FB paper

Fresh, running water	°C/°F	Time (min)
Double weight	Above 5/41	60

Do not wash ILFORD papers with some non-ILFORD papers which 'yellow' on prolonged washing, because this can cause the papers to have a bloom or haze over the black areas on the prints.

A washing aid is not needed when conventionally processing fibre base papers, but its use does reduce the final wash times, thus saving time and water. If a hardening fixer has been used, a washing aid is recommended as hardened prints take longer to wash. When using ILFORD WASHAID, wash prints for at least 5 minutes in running water before using the washing aid, then wash prints in running water for 20 minutes.

Washing aid

ILFORD washing aid	Dilution	°C/°F	Time (min)
Liquid ILFORD WASHAID	1+4	18–24/64–75	10

PROCESSING SHEET FILM

FP4 Plus, HP5 Plus, DELTA 100 Professional and ORTHO Copy Plus Sheet films can all be developed in a dish/tray using PQ UNIVERSAL developer 1+9 or 1+19 at 20°C/68°F. Development with dilution at 1+9 gives higher contrast but also an increase in granularity. Dilution 1+19 is recommended for pictorial contrast, Gbar 0.62, and lower grain but there is some loss of film speed and so for exposure a lower EI rating must be used.

PQ UNIVERSAL can also be used to develop the technical and sheet films of other manufacturers. Do not use PQ UNIVERSAL to process general purpose 35mm and roll film formats.

To develop sheet film formats in a dish/tray with PQ UNIVERSAL developer use the same techniques described above for dish/tray development of paper. We do not recommend the interleaving method for processing multiple sheets of film, even if great care is taken it may cause damage to the emulsion.

Film Development times

The development times given here are intended only as a guide and may be adjusted to suit individual preferences for density and contrast.

	EI	Time (min:sec)	Gbar
PQ UNIVERSAL 1+19 20°C/68°F			
FP4 Plus	64	4:00	0.62
HP5 Plus	320	4:30	0.62
Delta 100	80	4:00	0.62
ORTHO Copy Plus			
Daylight	25	4:00	0.62
Tungsten	12.5	4:00	0.62
PQ UNIVERSAL 1+9 20°C/68°F			
FP4 Plus	125–200	4:00–8:00	0.85–1.00
HP5 Plus	400–800	4:00–8:00	0.90–1.00
100 Delta	125–200	4:00–8:00	0.80–1.00
ORTHO Copy Plus			
Daylight	50–80	4:00–12:00	080–1.00
Tungsten	25–40	4:00–12:00	0.80–1.00

Developer Capacity for film

The following table gives the developing capacity of 1 litre of working strength developer.

	Dilution	20.3×25.4cm (8x10in) sheet film
PQ UNIVERSAL	1+9	10
	1+19	5

Stop

After development the film can be rinsed in water but we recommend that an acid stop bath is used such as ILFORD ILFOSTOP (with indicator dye) or ILFOSTOP PRO (without indicator dye). When tanks or dishes (trays) of process solutions are in use a stop bath immediately stops development and reduces carry over of excess developer into the fixer bath. This helps to maintain the activity and prolong the life of the fixer solution.

B&W PAPER DEVELOPERS

ILFORD Stop Bath	ILFOSTOP	ILFOSTOP PRO
Dilution	1+19	1+19
Temperature range	18–24°C (64–75°F)	18–24°C (64–75°F)
Time (seconds) at 20°C (68°F)	10	10
Capacity films/litre (unreplenished)	15 x 20.3x25.4cm (8x10in)	22 x 20.3x25.4cm (8x10in)

The process time given is the minimum required, if necessary a longer time may be used and should not cause any process problems provided it is not excessive.

Fix
The recommended fixers are ILFORD RAPID FIXER and ILFORD HYPAM liquid fixers and ILFORD ILFOFIX II powder fixer, all are non-hardening fixers.

ILFORD Fixer	ILFORD HYPAM & ILFORD RAPID FIXER	ILFORD ILFOFIX II
Dilution	1+4	stock
Temperature range	18–24°C (64–75°F)	18–24°C (64–75°F)
Time (mins) at 20°C (68°F)	2–5	4–8
Capacity films/litre (unreplenished)	24 x 20.3x25.4cm (8x10in)	24 x 20.3x25.4cm (8x10in)

Wash
When a non-hardening fixer has been used wash the films in running water for 5–10 minutes at a temperature within 5°C (9°F) of the process temperature.

Rinse
For a final rinse use ILFORD ILFOTOL wetting agent added to water, it helps the film to dry rapidly and evenly. Start by using 5ml per litre of rinse water (1+200), however the amount of ILFOTOL used may need some adjustment depending on the local water quality and drying method. Too little or too much wetting agent can lead to uneven drying. Remove excess rinse solution from the film before drying.

WORKING SOLUTION LIFE
BROMOPHEN stock solution should last for up to:-
6 months in full capped containers.
3 month in a half full tightly capped container.

Working strength MULTIGRADE developer, PQ UNIVERSAL and BROMOPHEN left in an open dish should not be kept for more than one working day. If stored in a tightly capped bottle they may last up to 24 hours.

STORAGE
Full unopened bottles of MULTIGRADE and PQ UNIVERSAL developer concentrates stored in cool conditions, 5–20°C, (41–68°F), will keep for 2 years. Once opened use the concentrate completely within six months and keep all bottles tightly sealed until used.

Unopened packets of BROMOPHEN powder stored in cool and dry conditions, 5–20°C, (41–68°F), will keep indefinitely. Once opened prepare the stock solution immediately.

AVAILABILITY AND CAPACITY
MULTIGRADE developer is available in bottles of 500ml, 1 litre, 2.5 litres, and 5 litres as well as a 10 litres "bag in box" carton.

A 1 litre bottle of MULTIGRADE developer makes enough working strength solution at 1+9 to process 1000 20.3x25.4cm (8x10in) sheets of RC paper or 500 20.3x25.4cm (8x10in) sheets of FB paper.

PQ UNIVERSAL is available in bottles of 500ml, 1 litre, and 5 litres.

A 1 litre bottle of PQ UNIVERSAL developer makes enough working strength solution at 1+9 to process 700 20.3x25.4cm (8x10in) sheets of RC paper or 450 20.3x25.4cm (8x10in) sheets of FB paper or 100 20.3x25.4cm (8x10in) sheet films.

BROMOPHEN is available in cartons of 1 and 5 litres.

A 1 litre carton of BROMOPHEN developer makes enough working strength solution at 1+3 to process 700 20.3x25.4cm (8x10in) sheets of RC paper or 450 20.3x25.4cm (8x10in) sheets of FB paper.

ILFORD
ILFOCHROME® CLASSIC
PROCESS P3
KIT 3.5

TO MAKE
POUR FAIRE
ERGIBT
PARA PREPARAR
VOOR

5 LITRES P3.5

EN Please consult Health & Safety instructions on this labels, and follow local regulations for disposal
Do not mix non-neutralised bleach with developer or fixer as formation of toxic sulphur dioxide would result

F Veuillez consulter les instructions de sécurité figurant sur les étiquettes et suivre les règlements locaux concernant
la rejet des produits usés.
Ne pas mélanger de blanchiment non neutralisé au révélateur ou au fixateur car il se produirait un dégagement
nocive de dioxyde de soufre.

D Bitte beachten Sie die Gesundheits und Sicherheitshinweise auf den Etiketten und befolgen Sie die lokal geltenden
Entsorgungsvorschriften.
Mischen Sie niemals unneutralisiertes Bleichbad mit Entwickler oder Fixierbad, denn würde sich Bildung von giftigem
Schwefeldioxid gas lösen.

E Consulte las instrucciones sobre salud y seguridad que figuran en las etiquetas y siga las normativas al productos conforme
a la normativa aplicable.
No mezcle blanqueador sin neutralizar con el revelador o fijador, ya que daría lugar a la formación de dióxido
de azufre tóxico.

NL Lees de gezondheids en veiligheidsinformatie op de etiketten en volg de lokale richtlijnen op voor de juiste afvoer
van al de verwerkte chemie.
Meng een ontkleurd bleekbad nooit met ontwikkelaar of fixeer, er kan dan een schadelijke ontstaan.

ADDITIONAL INFORMATION

HANDLING AND SAFETY PROCEDURES
The following cautions are supplied to you for your protection in compliance with the local Federal regulations and should be
followed when using all brands and types of photo chemicals in powder or liquid form.
CAUTION: The P3 processing kit contains sulphur, commonly used photographic chemicals in liquid form, and can produce sulfur
dioxide when mixed. Carefully read the warning on the individual containers, and observe all precautions printed on the
package label. These chemicals are not to be used by children, except under adult supervision. Promptly remove spilled solutions
from all surfaces in the darkroom. Handle the chemicals in a well ventilated area. Local exhaust ventilation must be provided in
situations when workplace ventilation does not provide 10 to 12 room air changes each hour.
Use care when handling all chemicals and preparing all processing solutions. Have an eye and face rinse available in the mixing
room at all times. The following precautions must be observed when handling ILFOCHROME CLASSIC P3 chemicals.
To avoid contact with skin and eyes, wear an apron, chemical resistant gloves, and use eye protection when preparing or handling
photographic chemicals in your home. Keep all the chemistry out of reach of children. If you store the chemistry in bottles, these
must be properly labelled or other special misuse.

FIRST AID INFORMATION
Eye contact: Immediately flush eyes with plenty of water for at least 15 minutes. GET MEDICAL ATTENTION.
Skin contact: Flush skin with water. If skin irritation occurs GET MEDICAL ATTENTION.
Ingestion: DO NOT INDUCE VOMITING. If conscious, drink one or two glasses of water.
               GET MEDICAL ATTENTION AT ONCE.
Inhalation: Remove to fresh air. If breathing is difficult GET MEDICAL ATTENTION AT ONCE.

ADDITIONAL MEDICAL INFORMATION (USA)
Call Poison Center at 1 - 800 - 842 - 9660 (24 hrs) for medical emergency information.

NEUTRALIZATION
Read the handling and safety procedures before working with liquid chemistry. Neutralization is
accomplished by adding 16 ounces of sodium bicarbonate to the entire product for each gallon of used bleach.
After the sodium bicarbonate is added the solution will stir vigorously. Use a container at least twice the
volume of the solutions to be neutralized.
DO NOT cover the container.

CONDITIONS OF SALE
ILFORD will replace this product if defective in manufacture, packaging or labeling and returned to ILFORD when one year of
purchase. Any warranties that may be implied by law are limited to the duration of this express warranty. Any and all liability for
incidental and consequential damages is disclaimed.
Some states do not allow limitations on how long an implied warranty lasts and some states do not allow the exclusion or limitation
of incidental or consequential damages so the above limitations or exclusions may not apply to you. This warranty gives you
specific legal rights and you may also have other rights which vary from state to state.

ILFORD® is a trademark of ILFORD Imaging Switzerland GmbH
ILFORD Imaging Switzerland GmbH, CH-1723 Marly 1

116F5X/85

108

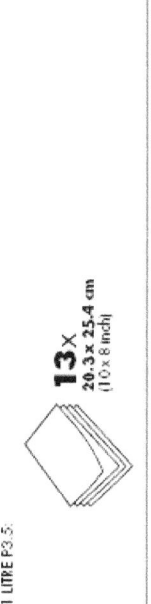

Darkroom Data Guide

MIXING INSTRUCTIONS / INSTRUCTIONS DE MELANGE / LÖSUNGSVORSCHRIFT / INSTRUCCION DE MEZCLA / AANZETINSTRUCTIE

DE 3.5 — DEVELOPER / REVELATEUR / ENTWICKLER / REVELADOR / ONTWIKKELAAR

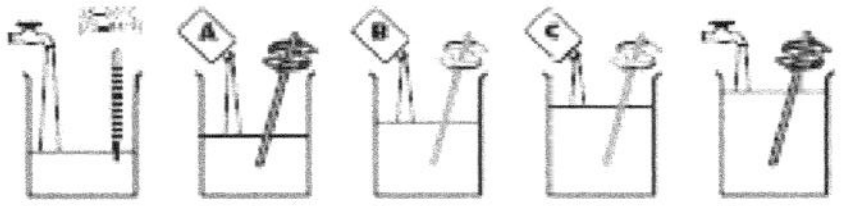

	H_2O	Part A	Part B	Part C	H_2O
1 litre DE 3.5	400ml	250ml	160ml	160ml	→ 1 litre
2 litres DE 3.5	800ml	500ml	200ml	200ml	→ 2litres
5 litres DE 3.5	2 litres	1.25 litre	500ml	500ml	→ 5litres

BL 3.5 — BLEACH / BLANCHIMENT / BLEICHBAD / BLANQUEADOR / BLEEKBAD

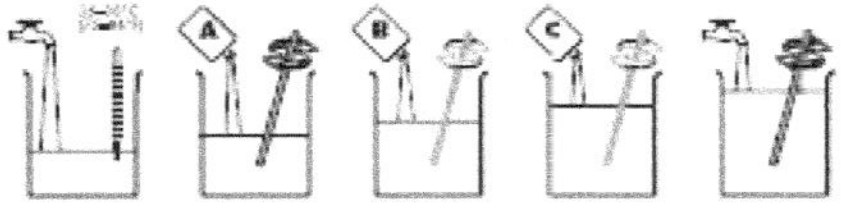

	H_2O	Part A	Part B	Part C	H_2O
1 litre BL 3.5	400ml	200ml	100ml	100ml	→ 1 litre
2 litres BL 3.5	800ml	400ml	200ml	200ml	→ 2litres
5 litres BL 3.5	2 litres	2 × 500ml	500ml	500ml	→ 5litres

FX 3.5 — FIXER / FIXATEUR / FIXIERBAD / FIJADOR / FIXEER

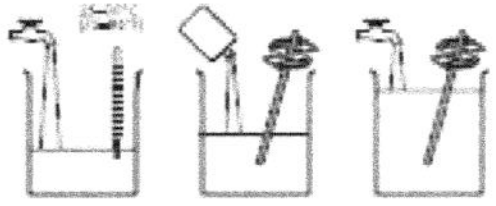

	H_2O			H_2O
1 litre FX 3.5	500ml	400ml		→ 1 litre
2 litres FX 3.5	1 litre	800ml		→ 2litres
5 litres FX 3.5	2.5 litres	2 litres		→ 5litres

Working strength / Solution de travail / Gebrauchslösung / Selector para uso / Gebruiksoplossing

STORAGE / STOCKAGE / LAGERUNG / ALMACENAJE / OPSLAG
10–20°C (50–68°F)

Concentrate / Concentrés / Konzentrate / Concentrado / Concentraat

---

PROCESSING SEQUENCE / SEQUENCE DE TRAITEMENT / VERARBEITUNGSSEQUENZ / SECUENCIA DE PROCESO / PROCESGEGEVENS

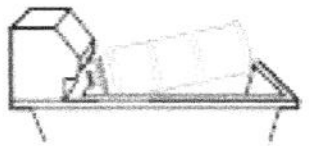

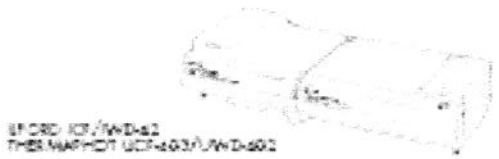

ILFOCHROME CLASSIC CLM.1K / CPS.1K			ILFOCHROME CLASSIC CLM.1K / CPS.1K
Temperature / Température / Temperatur	24°C (75°F)	30°C (86°F)	32°C – 34°C (90°F – 94°F)
Development / Développement / Entwicklung	3 min	2-3 min	2 min
Rinse / Rinçage / Spülen	30 s	30 s	—
Bleach / Blanchiment / Bleichbad	3 min	2-3 min	2 min
Fix / Fixage / Fixierbad	3 min	2 min	2 min
Wash / Lavage / Wässerung	3 min	2 min	4 min
Dry / Séchage / Trocknung	50-70°C (120-160°F)	50-70°C (120-160°F)	50-70°C (120-160°F)

Note: Adjust time or temperature to optimise your results.

1 LITRE P3.5:

13× 20.3 × 25.4 cm (10 × 8 inch)

109

Appendix

Darkroom Data Guide

Conversion Tables mm to inches

mm	Inches	mm	Inches	mm	Inches	mm	inches
1.00	0.04	51.00	2.01	110.00	4.34	620.00	24.42
2.00	0.08	52.00	2.05	120.00	4.73	630.00	24.81
3.00	0.12	53.00	2.09	130.00	5.12	640.00	25.20
4.00	0.16	54.00	2.13	140.00	5.52	650.00	25.60
5.00	0.20	55.00	2.17	150.00	5.91	660.00	25.99
6.00	0.24	56.00	2.21	160.00	6.30	670.00	26.39
7.00	0.28	57.00	2.25	170.00	6.70	680.00	26.78
8.00	0.32	58.00	2.29	180.00	7.09	690.00	27.17
9.00	0.36	59.00	2.33	190.00	7.49	700.00	27.57
10.00	0.40	60.00	2.37	200.00	7.88	710.00	27.96
11.00	0.44	61.00	2.41	210.00	8.27	720.00	28.35
12.00	0.48	62.00	2.45	220.00	8.67	730.00	28.75
13.00	0.52	63.00	2.49	230.00	9.06	740.00	29.14
14.00	0.56	64.00	2.52	240.00	9.45	750.00	29.54
15.00	0.60	65.00	2.56	250.00	9.85	760.00	29.93
16.00	0.63	66.00	2.60	260.00	10.24	770.00	30.32
17.00	0.67	67.00	2.64	270.00	10.64	780.00	30.72
18.00	0.71	68.00	2.68	280.00	11.03	790.00	31.11
19.00	0.75	69.00	2.72	290.00	11.42	800.00	31.50
20.00	0.79	70.00	2.76	300.00	11.82	810.00	31.90
21.00	0.83	71.00	2.80	310.00	12.21	820.00	32.29
22.00	0.87	72.00	2.84	320.00	12.60	830.00	32.69
23.00	0.91	73.00	2.88	330.00	13.00	840.00	33.08
24.00	0.95	74.00	2.92	340.00	13.39	850.00	33.47
25.00	0.99	75.00	2.96	350.00	13.79	860.00	33.87
26.00	1.03	76.00	3.00	360.00	14.18	870.00	34.26
27.00	1.07	77.00	3.04	370.00	14.57	880.00	34.65
28.00	1.11	78.00	3.08	380.00	14.97	890.00	35.05
29.00	1.15	79.00	3.12	390.00	15.36	900.00	35.44
30.00	1.19	80.00	3.15	400.00	15.75	910.00	35.84
31.00	1.23	81.00	3.19	410.00	16.15	920.00	36.23
32.00	1.26	82.00	3.23	420.00	16.54	930.00	36.62
33.00	1.30	83.00	3.27	430.00	16.94	940.00	37.02
34.00	1.34	84.00	3.31	440.00	17.33	950.00	37.41
35.00	1.38	85.00	3.35	450.00	17.72	960.00	37.80
36.00	1.42	86.00	3.39	460.00	18.12	970.00	38.20
37.00	1.46	87.00	3.43	470.00	18.51	980.00	38.59
38.00	1.50	88.00	3.47	480.00	18.90	990.00	38.99
39.00	1.54	89.00	3.51	490.00	19.30	1000.00	39.38
40.00	1.58	90.00	3.55	500.00	19.69	1010.00	39.77
41.00	1.62	91.00	3.59	510.00	20.09	1020.00	40.17
42.00	1.66	92.00	3.63	520.00	20.48	1030.00	40.56
43.00	1.70	93.00	3.67	530.00	20.87	1040.00	40.95
44.00	1.74	94.00	3.71	540.00	21.27	1050.00	41.35
45.00	1.78	95.00	3.75	550.00	21.66	1060.00	41.74
46.00	1.82	96.00	3.78	560.00	22.05	1070.00	42.14
47.00	1.86	97.00	3.82	570.00	22.45	1080.00	42.53
48.00	1.89	98.00	3.86	580.00	22.84	1090.00	42.92
49.00	1.93	99.00	3.90	590.00	23.24	1100.00	43.32
50.00	1.97	100.00	3.94	600.00	23.63	1110.00	43.71

Darkroom Data Guide

Conversion Tables inches to mm

Inches	mm	Inches	mm	Inches	mm	Inches	mm
0.10	2.54	5.10	129.53	10.10	256.51	16.00	406.35
0.20	5.08	5.20	132.07	10.20	259.05	17.00	431.75
0.30	7.62	5.30	134.61	10.30	261.59	18.00	457.15
0.40	10.16	5.40	137.15	10.40	264.13	19.00	482.54
0.50	12.70	5.50	139.69	10.50	266.67	20.00	507.94
0.60	15.24	5.60	142.23	10.60	269.21	21.00	533.34
0.70	17.78	5.70	144.77	10.70	271.75	22.00	558.74
0.80	20.32	5.80	147.31	10.80	274.29	23.00	584.13
0.90	22.86	5.90	149.85	10.90	276.83	24.00	609.53
1.00	25.40	6.00	152.39	11.00	279.37	25.00	634.93
1.10	27.94	6.10	154.93	11.10	281.91	26.00	660.32
1.20	30.48	6.20	157.47	11.20	284.45	27.00	685.72
1.30	33.02	6.30	160.00	11.30	286.99	28.00	711.12
1.40	35.56	6.40	162.54	11.40	289.53	29.00	736.51
1.50	38.10	6.50	165.08	11.50	292.07	30.00	761.91
1.60	40.64	6.60	167.62	11.60	294.61	31.00	787.31
1.70	43.18	6.70	170.16	11.70	297.15	32.00	812.70
1.80	45.72	6.80	172.70	11.80	299.69	33.00	838.10
1.90	48.26	6.90	175.24	11.90	302.23	34.00	863.50
2.00	50.80	7.00	177.78	12.00	304.77	35.00	888.89
2.10	53.34	7.10	180.32	12.10	307.31	36.00	914.29
2.20	55.88	7.20	182.86	12.20	309.85	37.00	939.69
2.30	58.42	7.30	185.40	12.30	312.39	38.00	965.08
2.40	60.96	7.40	187.94	12.40	314.93	39.00	990.48
2.50	63.50	7.50	190.48	12.50	317.47	40.00	1015.88
2.60	66.04	7.60	193.02	12.60	320.00	41.00	1041.27
2.70	68.58	7.70	195.56	12.70	322.54	42.00	1066.67
2.80	71.12	7.80	198.10	12.80	325.08	43.00	1092.07
2.90	73.66	7.90	200.64	12.90	327.62	44.00	1117.47
3.00	76.20	8.00	203.18	13.00	330.16	45.00	1142.86
3.10	78.74	8.10	205.72	13.10	332.70	46.00	1168.26
3.20	81.27	8.20	208.26	13.20	335.24	47.00	1193.66
3.30	83.81	8.30	210.80	13.30	337.78	48.00	1219.05
3.40	86.35	8.40	213.34	13.40	340.32	49.00	1244.45
3.50	88.89	8.50	215.88	13.50	342.86	50.00	1269.85
3.60	91.43	8.60	218.42	13.60	345.40	51.00	1295.24
3.70	93.97	8.70	220.96	13.70	347.94	52.00	1320.64
3.80	96.51	8.80	223.50	13.80	350.48	53.00	1346.04
3.90	99.05	8.90	226.04	13.90	353.02	54.00	1371.43
4.00	101.59	9.00	228.58	14.00	355.56	55.00	1396.83
4.10	104.13	9.10	231.12	14.10	358.10	56.00	1422.23
4.20	106.67	9.20	233.66	14.20	360.64	57.00	1447.62
4.30	109.21	9.30	236.20	14.30	363.18	58.00	1473.02
4.40	111.75	9.40	238.74	14.40	365.72	59.00	1498.42
4.50	114.29	9.50	241.27	14.50	368.26	60.00	1523.81
4.60	116.83	9.60	243.81	14.60	370.80	61.00	1549.21
4.70	119.37	9.70	246.35	14.70	373.34	62.00	1574.61
4.80	121.91	9.80	248.89	14.80	375.88	63.00	1600.00
4.90	124.45	9.90	251.43	14.90	378.42	64.00	1625.40
5.00	126.99	10.00	253.97	15.00	380.96	65.00	1650.80

Darkroom Data Guide

Conversion Tables Litres to UK and US gallons

Litres	UK Gallons	US Gallons	ML	UK Gallons	US Gallons	ML	UK Gallons	US Gallons
1	0.22	0.26	51	11.22	13.47	150	33.00	39.63
2	0.44	0.53	52	11.44	13.74	200	44.00	52.83
3	0.66	0.79	53	11.66	14.00	250	55.00	66.04
4	0.88	1.06	54	11.88	14.27	300	66.00	79.25
5	1.10	1.32	55	12.10	14.53	350	76.99	92.46
6	1.32	1.59	56	12.32	14.79	400	87.99	105.67
7	1.54	1.85	57	12.54	15.06	450	98.99	118.88
8	1.76	2.11	58	12.76	15.32	500	109.99	132.09
9	1.98	2.38	59	12.98	15.59	550	120.99	145.29
10	2.20	2.64	60	13.20	15.85	600	131.99	158.50
11	2.42	2.91	61	13.42	16.11	650	142.98	171.71
12	2.64	3.17	62	13.64	16.38	700	153.98	184.92
13	2.86	3.43	63	13.86	16.64	750	164.98	198.13
14	3.08	3.70	64	14.08	16.91	800	175.98	211.34
15	3.30	3.96	65	14.30	17.17	850	186.98	224.55
16	3.52	4.23	66	14.52	17.44	900	197.98	237.75
17	3.74	4.49	67	14.74	17.70	950	208.98	250.96
18	3.96	4.76	68	14.96	17.96	1000	219.97	264.17
19	4.18	5.02	69	15.18	18.23	1500	329.96	396.26
20	4.40	5.28	70	15.40	18.49	2000	439.94	528.34
21	4.62	5.55	71	15.62	18.76	2500	549.93	660.43
22	4.84	5.81	72	15.84	19.02	3000	659.91	792.52
23	5.06	6.08	73	16.06	19.28	3500	769.90	924.60
24	5.28	6.34	74	16.28	19.55	4000	879.88	1056.69
25	5.50	6.60	75	16.50	19.81	4500	989.87	1188.77
26	5.72	6.87	76	16.72	20.08	5000	1099.85	1320.86
27	5.94	7.13	77	16.94	20.34	5500	1209.84	1452.95
28	6.16	7.40	78	17.16	20.61	6000	1319.82	1585.03
29	6.38	7.66	79	17.38	20.87	6500	1429.80	1717.12
30	6.60	7.93	80	17.60	21.13	7000	1539.79	1849.20
31	6.82	8.19	81	17.82	21.40	7500	1649.77	1981.29
32	7.04	8.45	82	18.04	21.66	8000	1759.76	2113.38
33	7.26	8.72	83	18.26	21.93	8500	1869.74	2245.46
34	7.48	8.98	84	18.48	22.19	9000	1979.73	2377.55
35	7.70	9.25	85	18.70	22.45	9500	2089.71	2509.63
36	7.92	9.51	86	18.92	22.72	10000	2199.70	2641.72
37	8.14	9.77	87	19.14	22.98	10500	2309.68	2773.81
38	8.36	10.04	88	19.36	23.25	11000	2419.67	2905.89
39	8.58	10.30	89	19.58	23.51	11500	2529.65	3037.98
40	8.80	10.57	90	19.80	23.78	12000	2639.63	3170.06
41	9.02	10.83	91	20.02	24.04	12500	2749.62	3302.15
42	9.24	11.10	92	20.24	24.30	13000	2859.60	3434.24
43	9.46	11.36	93	20.46	24.57	13500	2969.59	3566.32
44	9.68	11.62	94	20.68	24.83	14000	3079.57	3698.41
45	9.90	11.89	95	20.90	25.10	14500	3189.56	3830.49
46	10.12	12.15	96	21.12	25.36	15000	3299.54	3962.58
47	10.34	12.42	97	21.34	25.62	15500	3409.53	4094.67
48	10.56	12.68	98	21.56	25.89	16000	3519.51	4226.75
49	10.78	12.94	99	21.78	26.15	16500	3629.50	4358.84
50	11.00	13.21	100	22.00	26.42	17000	3739.48	4490.92

Darkroom Data Guide

Conversion Tables ml to UK and US Fluid Ounces

ML	UK fl.oz	US fl.oz	ML	UK fl.oz	US fl.oz	ML	UK fl.oz	US fl.oz
1	0.04	0.03	51	1.80	1.72	150	5.28	5.07
2	0.08	0.07	52	1.84	1.76	200	7.04	6.76
3	0.11	0.10	53	1.87	1.79	250	8.80	8.45
4	0.15	0.14	54	1.91	1.83	300	10.56	10.14
5	0.18	0.17	55	1.94	1.86	350	12.32	11.83
6	0.22	0.20	56	1.98	1.89	400	14.08	13.53
7	0.25	0.24	57	2.01	1.93	450	15.84	15.22
8	0.29	0.27	58	2.05	1.96	500	17.60	16.91
9	0.32	0.30	59	2.08	2.00	550	19.36	18.60
10	0.36	0.34	60	2.12	2.03	600	21.12	20.29
11	0.39	0.37	61	2.15	2.06	650	22.88	21.98
12	0.43	0.41	62	2.19	2.10	700	24.64	23.67
13	0.46	0.44	63	2.22	2.13	750	26.40	25.36
14	0.50	0.47	64	2.26	2.16	800	28.16	27.05
15	0.53	0.51	65	2.29	2.20	850	29.92	28.74
16	0.57	0.54	66	2.33	2.23	900	31.68	30.43
17	0.60	0.57	67	2.36	2.27	950	33.44	32.12
18	0.64	0.61	68	2.40	2.30	1000	35.20	33.81
19	0.67	0.64	69	2.43	2.33	1500	52.80	50.72
20	0.71	0.68	70	2.47	2.37	2000	70.40	67.63
21	0.74	0.71	71	2.50	2.40	2500	88.00	84.54
22	0.78	0.74	72	2.54	2.43	3000	105.60	101.44
23	0.81	0.78	73	2.57	2.47	3500	123.20	118.35
24	0.85	0.81	74	2.61	2.50	4000	140.80	135.26
25	0.88	0.85	75	2.64	2.54	4500	158.40	152.16
26	0.92	0.88	76	2.68	2.57	5000	176.00	169.07
27	0.96	0.91	77	2.72	2.60	5500	193.60	185.98
28	0.99	0.95	78	2.75	2.64	6000	211.20	202.88
29	1.03	0.98	79	2.79	2.67	6500	228.80	219.79
30	1.06	1.01	80	2.82	2.71	7000	246.40	236.70
31	1.10	1.05	81	2.86	2.74	7500	264.00	253.61
32	1.13	1.08	82	2.89	2.77	8000	281.60	270.51
33	1.17	1.12	83	2.93	2.81	8500	299.20	287.42
34	1.20	1.15	84	2.96	2.84	9000	316.80	304.33
35	1.24	1.18	85	3.00	2.87	9500	334.40	321.23
36	1.27	1.22	86	3.03	2.91	10000	352.00	338.14
37	1.31	1.25	87	3.07	2.94	10500	369.60	355.05
38	1.34	1.28	88	3.10	2.98	11000	387.20	371.95
39	1.38	1.32	89	3.14	3.01	11500	404.80	388.86
40	1.41	1.35	90	3.17	3.04	12000	422.40	405.77
41	1.45	1.39	91	3.21	3.08	12500	440.00	422.68
42	1.48	1.42	92	3.24	3.11	13000	457.60	439.58
43	1.52	1.45	93	3.28	3.14	13500	475.20	456.49
44	1.55	1.49	94	3.31	3.18	14000	492.80	473.40
45	1.59	1.52	95	3.35	3.21	14500	510.40	490.30
46	1.62	1.56	96	3.38	3.25	15000	528.00	507.21
47	1.66	1.59	97	3.42	3.28	15500	545.60	524.12
48	1.69	1.62	98	3.45	3.31	16000	563.20	541.02
49	1.73	1.66	99	3.49	3.35	16500	580.80	557.93
50	1.76	1.69	100	3.52	3.38	17000	598.40	574.84

Darkroom Data Guide

Conversion Tables Degrees F to Degrees Celcius

Deg F	Deg C	Deg F	Deg C	Deg C	Deg F	Deg C	Deg F
32	0.00	83	28.34	0	32.00	51	123.80
33	0.56	84	28.89	1	33.80	52	125.60
34	1.12	85	29.45	2	35.60	53	127.40
35	1.67	86	30.00	3	37.40	54	129.20
36	2.23	87	30.56	4	39.20	55	131.00
37	2.78	88	31.12	5	41.00	56	132.80
38	3.34	89	31.67	6	42.80	57	134.60
39	3.89	90	32.23	7	44.60	58	136.40
40	4.45	91	32.78	8	46.40	59	138.20
41	5.00	92	33.34	9	48.20	60	140.00
42	5.56	93	33.89	10	50.00	61	141.80
43	6.12	94	34.45	11	51.80	62	143.60
44	6.67	95	35.00	12	53.60	63	145.40
45	7.23	96	35.56	13	55.40	64	147.20
46	7.78	97	36.12	14	57.20	65	149.00
47	8.34	98	36.67	15	59.00	66	150.80
48	8.89	99	37.23	16	60.80	67	152.60
49	9.45	100	37.78	17	62.60	68	154.40
50	10.00	101	38.34	18	64.40	69	156.20
51	10.56	102	38.89	19	66.20	70	158.00
52	11.12	103	39.45	20	68.00	71	159.80
53	11.67	104	40.00	21	69.80	72	161.60
54	12.23	105	40.56	22	71.60	73	163.40
55	12.78	106	41.12	23	73.40	74	165.20
56	13.34	107	41.67	24	75.20	75	167.00
57	13.89	108	42.23	25	77.00	76	168.80
58	14.45	109	42.78	26	78.80	77	170.60
59	15.00	110	43.34	27	80.60	78	172.40
60	15.56	111	43.89	28	82.40	79	174.20
61	16.12	112	44.45	29	84.20	80	176.00
62	16.67	113	45.00	30	86.00	81	177.80
63	17.23	114	45.56	31	87.80	82	179.60
64	17.78	115	46.12	32	89.60	83	181.40
65	18.34	116	46.67	33	91.40	84	183.20
66	18.89	117	47.23	34	93.20	85	185.00
67	19.45	118	47.78	35	95.00	86	186.80
68	20.00	119	48.34	36	96.80	87	188.60
69	20.56	120	48.89	37	98.60	88	190.40
70	21.12	121	49.45	38	100.40	89	192.20
71	21.67	122	50.00	39	102.20	90	194.00
72	22.23	123	50.56	40	104.00	91	195.80
73	22.78	124	51.12	41	105.80	92	197.60
74	23.34	125	51.67	42	107.60	93	199.40
75	23.89	126	52.23	43	109.40	94	201.20
76	24.45	127	52.78	44	111.20	95	203.00
77	25.00	128	53.34	45	113.00	96	204.80
78	25.56	129	53.89	46	114.80	97	206.60
79	26.12	130	54.45	47	116.60	98	208.40
80	26.67	131	55.00	48	118.40	99	210.20
81	27.23	132	55.56	49	120.20	100	212.00
82	27.78	133	56.12	50	122.00	101	213.80

Useful Chemical Aids

Product	Supplier	Comments
Film Cleaner	Tetenal Fotospeed Speedibrews	Removes fingerprints, grease etc. from films
Farmers Reducer	Tetenal Fotospeed	Corrects overexposure/overdevelopment in b&w films and prints
Chromium Intensifier	Fotospeed	Supplied as a single liquid concentrate designed to intensify thin B&W negatives. The negative is bleached back in CI10 (diluted 1+4 with water) and then redeveloped in PRINT developer. The image will return stronger. The process can be repeated a few times to maximise intensification. There is no need to refix the negative - just wash thoroughly.
Exargent	Tetenal	For the removal of silver stains e.g. from clothes and diochroic fog from films
Anti Newton Ring spray	Tetenal	Prevents Newtons rings on glass surfaces
Anti-static spray	Tetenal	Stops and eliminates static charges
Anti dust	Tetenal	Prevents dust from settling
Colourlab cleaner	Tetenal	Alkaline cleaner to remove developer stains or tar from processing equipment
Protectan spray	Tetenal	Protects developers and other photographic solutions from oxidation
Mirasol anti static liquid	Tetenal	Antistatic wetting agent with anti-bacteria action. Dilution: 1 + 400
Raw chemicals	Arem Direct Silverprint	Photographic quality chemicals for making photographic processing solutions to your own formulae
Anti Fog Agent	Silverprint	Add to developer to reduce base fog with aging papers
Algae Killer	Agfa	Claimed to be the most effective algae killer known. Not available by post

These chemicals are available from most good darkroom suppliers

Darkroom Data Guide

Darkroom Data Log

Date	File Ref	Film	ISO	Neg No	Neg Size	Exposure time secs	f stop No	Y	M	C	Column height	Paper Type	Print Ref	Comments

117

Darkroom Data Guide

Darkroom Data Log

Date	File Ref	Film	ISO	Neg No	Neg Size	Exposure time secs	f stop No	Y	M	C	Column height	Paper Type	Print Ref	Comments

Darkroom Data Guide

Darkroom Data Log

Date	File Ref	Film	ISO	Neg No	Neg Size	Exposure time secs	f stop No	Y	M	C	Column height	Paper Type	Print Ref	Comments

Darkroom Data Guide

Darkroom Data Log

Date	File Ref	Film	ISO	Neg No	Neg Size	Exposure time secs	f stop No	Y	M	C	Column height	Paper Type	Print Ref	Comments

Darkroom Data Guide

Notes

www.ingramcontent.com/pod-product-compliance
Lightning Source LLC
Chambersburg PA
CBHW051325170526
45166CB00002B/694